Formation Activities and Catholic Seminarians

A Practical Theological Study of their Impact on Subsequent Perseverance in Ministry

Rev. Alfredo I. Hernández

En Route Books and Media, LLC
St. Louis, MO

ENROUTE
Make the time

En Route Books and Media, LLC
5705 Rhodes Avenue
St. Louis, MO 63109

Cover credit: TJ Burdick

Library of Congress Control Number: 2020939671

ISBN-13: 978-1-952464-10-2

DEDICATION

This work would not have been possible without those who were my first formators in the Christian life and who taught me all about perseverance in vocational commitment, my parents.

To my father, Mr. Julio Luis Hernández, who died in 2006, and to my mother, Mrs. Loló Villa Hernández, I dedicate this work with love and gratitude for their example of joyful faithfulness.

Table of Contents

Acknowledgments i

Introduction 1

What is the purpose of seminary formation? 2

A word about practical theology and methodology 4

Why is this study relevant?................................... 8

What did the study try to accomplish? 11

Chapter 1: Perseverance in Ministry: Why Does It Matter?.. 13

What is perseverance?... 13

New Testament.. 15

The Fathers.. 19

The Scholastics.. 23

Protestant Reformation 24

Trent.. 25

Pope Pius XI 26

Vatican II 28
Post-Conciliar Theology 31
Perseverance for the sake of the People of God 34
Chapter 2: A Study of Seminary Formation Programs 37
What programs? 37
Clinical Pastoral Education (CPE) 38
Spirituality or propaedeutic year 50
Pastoral-year internship 59
Priestly fraternity groups 72
Institute for Priestly Formation 80
Language Immersion Programs 85
Theological reflection 92
Chapter 3: Seminary Formation Activities: What Impact on Perseverance? 99
Introduction to the research process 99
Development of the mailing list 101
Development of the questionnaire 102
Data collection process 104
Concern about the sample size and number of responses 105
Empirical-theological data analysis 107
Overall evaluation of the formation activities 111

Impact of the formation activities on the totality of seminary experience 119
Impact of the formation activities on understanding of priestly identity 121
Impact of the formation activities on attitude toward the commitment to celibacy 128
Another way to visualize results: Net Impact Score 130
Narrative responses 137
CPE 138
Spirituality or Propaedeutic Year 139
Pastoral-year internship 140
Institute for Priestly Formation (IPF) 142
Conclusion 145
Bibliography 155

Acknowledgments

I need to express gratitude to the faculty and staff of the Greenwich School of Theology and North-West University (Potchefstroom Campus), who supported me throughout the doctoral research that provided the basis of this book. Father Joseph O'Hanlon and Professor F.P. Kruger, who served as Promoter and Co-promoter, respectively, were extremely supportive and encouraging throughout my research, at the same time challenging me to give the best of myself. At the same time, the support of Mrs. Peg Evans and Mrs. Tienie Buys was invaluable; they were always available to answer any question. I need to offer a special mention of gratitude and a word of prayer for Professor Fritz de Wet, who had initially been assigned as Co-promoter and passed away unexpectedly just as my project was beginning.

I also need to offer thanks to the faculty and staff of St. Vincent de Paul Regional Seminary, in Boynton

Beach, Florida, where I am on the formation faculty, teach, and serve as Acting President-Rector after having served as Vice-Rector and Academic Dean. My colleagues supported me and were patient with me throughout this journey. The Rector, now at the time this book goes to print, Bishop-Elect David Toups, encouraged me constantly. Mr. Art Quinn, Librarian, was of invaluable assistance whenever I have needed any help. Dr. S. Mary Krysiak Bittár, Director of Institutional Research and Effectiveness, offered many useful suggestions. Father Llane Briese, Director of Non-Resident Students, offered me great help in editing and proofing the dissertation, as did Father John Horn, SJ, in reviewing this text. The Registrar, Mrs. Alicia Rueff, was patient with her supervisor whenever I had to close my door and say: "I am a doctoral student now." Also, Mrs. Barbara Joseph, Receptionist, and Mrs. Joan Bien, a dear volunteer, were of tremendous help when it came time to do mailings.

Dr. S. Mary Krysiak Bittár's research methodology students at Loyola University in the summer of 2017 afforded me great help with a test version of the survey, as did a group of alumni of my seminary. My nephew, Mr. Kevin Hernández, Enterprise Data Science and Analytics Manager for CableOne, assisted me in the analysis of the data, and he also suggested the use of the Net Impact Score and coined the expression. To all those who completed the surveys, and to the seminary pro-fessionals who responded to questionnaires about their programmes (Father John Horn, SJ; Sister Leanne Hubbard, SND; Sister Mary Regina Robbins, SND; Msgr. Michael Muhr; Father Jim Thermos), many thanks.

I owe particular gratitude to my brother priests and those with whom I have worked in seminary formation, in one way or another. This work is offered with the hope that our shared presbyterate may be more joyful and fruitful each day, for the good of the people to whom we seek to give ourselves with love. I offer this work with a special prayer for my Bishop, Most Reverend Gerald M. Barbarito, who constantly prays and works so that the priests of the Diocese of Palm Beach may be able to serve their people better.

As I was completing my doctoral dissertation, reports of sexual abuse by clergy, most in the distant past, but some more recent, once again hit the news, in the US and around the world. The role of Bishops and of the Holy See in the handling of reports has been a particular aspect of the ensuing scandal. It was beyond the scope of my work to offer analysis of these events. Also, as this book was being prepared for publication in the late winter and spring of 2020, the world and our country have been shaken by the global COVID-19 pandemic and by protests calling for racial justice. This unprecedented confluence of phenomena present new and extraordinary challenges for the Church and for seminary formators and provide a backdrop for this study. Clearly, it is more urgent than ever for seminaries to prepare seminarians for faithful and committed ministry as priests, prepared to serve lovingly and effectively in an ever-changing reality.

Father Alfredo I. Hernández

June 19, 2020
Solemnity of the Sacred Heart of Jesus
World Day of Prayer for the Sanctification of Priests

Introduction

What can we seminary formators, Bishops, and others involved in the formation of seminarians do to help the men who are ordained from our seminaries to be joyful and fruitful as priests and persevere in ministry? In more than two decades as a full-time or adjunct faculty member at St. Vincent de Paul Regional Seminary in Boynton Beach, Florida, this question has often been on my mind. It became a central question for my doctoral research dissertation, *Formation Activities and Catholic Seminarians: A Practical Theological Study of Their Impact on Subsequent Perseverance in Ministry* (Hernández, 2019), after which I've entitled this book. My hope in the present text is to offer some of the results of this exercise in practical theology in a way that will be accessible to many who are involved in seminary formation in order to contribute to decision-making for the good of seminarians and future priests and for the good of the Church in the United States and beyond.

What is the purpose of seminary formation?

Catholic theological seminaries in the United States and around the world invest a great deal of resources, both the financial resources of the dioceses which send seminarians to them as well as the time and effort of the seminarians and the seminary staff, into a variety of programs (Association of Theological Schools, 2016). All of these have as their aim to help seminarians to prepare to be, as priests, shepherds who can truly represent Jesus Christ. The *Program of Priestly Formation* (*PPF*), 5th Edition, the guiding document for the formation of Catholic priests in the United States, states that priests are called to represent Christ for the members of the Church. The document expresses the conviction that grace is given at ordination, and at the same time, is clear about the need for the priest "to develop the knowledge and skills to teach and preach well, to celebrate the sacraments both properly and prayerfully, and to respond to people's needs as well as to take initiatives in the community that holy leadership requires" (USCCB, 2006, p. 77, §238). The *PPF* also indicates that seminarians, before ordination as transitional deacons, are to be prepared to make a "permanent commitment" to ordained ministry (USCCB, 2006, p. 94, §285).

Grace and personal effort are in constant tension; seminary formation needs to assist seminarians to recognize that they need both God's help and their own effort to become good and faithful priests. Dorothy Day (1945), writing in a different context, indicated that total faith in God and the hard work that the journey towards holiness requires should not be put in opposition to each other. Expressed in terms of the efforts to resolve the centuries-old debate between Lutherans and Catholics about the relationship between grace and human effort, the *Joint Declaration on Justification* between the Catholic Church and the Lutheran World Federation (1999:§20) states: "When Catholics say that persons 'cooperate' in preparing for and accepting justification by consenting to God's justifying action, they see such personal consent as itself an effect of grace, not as an action arising from innate human abilities." In my research, I presupposed the aid of God's grace but tried to focus on the various formational activities—both required and optional—undertaken by seminarians, hoping to determine whether they assist the priest, after ordination, to be faithful to his commitment.

A word about practical theology and methodology

My research was a work in practical theology. While all the aspects of the practical theological approaches which were used will not be discussed at every stage, it is helpful to discuss the methodology which structured the project. Ballard and Pritchard (1996, p.74) recognize the roots of what they describe as the "pastoral cycle" in the "see-judge-act" methodology of Catholic Action in the mid-twentieth century, as well as in liberation theology. They describe the pastoral cycle in four steps: "experience" — the current reality, affected by outside forces; "exploration," — the analysis of the current reality, using various means; "reflection" — theological consideration of the reality that has been analysed: "Perceptions, beliefs and values face the challenge of being in touch with contemporary realities;" "action" — specific proposals and efforts to effect change (Ballard & Pritchard, 1996, pp. 77–78). Osmer (2008, pp. vii, 11) presents this same cycle as four "tasks" for practical theology: "descriptive-empirical," "interpretative," "normative," and "pragmatic." While I followed the methodology of Van der Ven (1998), Osmer's (2008) descriptors for the phases or tasks of practical theology (and others' similar descriptors) should be kept in mind. Together with the effort to describe the history and the status of Catholic theologies of the priesthood, as well as the formation activities for seminarians being studied, I proposed an interpretation of these theologies and programs (including their normative elements), as well as of the data from the survey conducted, and this process led to specific recommendations for change in practice.

The nature of Catholic theological formation is such that it is important to consider carefully the purposes of that formation, as expressed in the tradition and in magisterial documents. In a sense, the "dialogue" which Ballard and Pritchard (1996, pp. 82–83) describe as part of their model has to include, in this case, dialogue with the tradition and with the magisterium, so that "practical theology draws on the tradition" (Ballard & Pritchard, 1996, p. 84).

Like other practical theologians, Van der Ven describes four "phases of the experience cycle: perception, experimentation, examination, and assessment" (1998, p. 112), but these have a particular empirical focus. It is this empirical aspect that led me to adapt his methodology, while borrowing from some of the others mentioned. Van der Ven applies the empirical focus to practical theology, as he articulates the steps of the "empirical-theological cycle": "1. development of problem and goal, 2. induction, 3. deduction, 4. testing, and 5. evaluation" (van der Ven, 1998, p. 114). He affirms the "complementarity of qualitative and quantitative empirical methodology" (van der Ven, 1998, p. 106).

These detailed steps of my research will be summarized in this text in three stages. First, we will discuss the importance of perseverance in priesthood: why does remaining in ministry for life matter to the priest himself and to the Church? Second, I will offer a study of several formational activities seminaries and dioceses in the United States require or encourage their seminarians to use. These programs are Clinical Pastoral Education (CPE), spirituality or propaedeutic year, the pastoral-year internship, priestly fraternity groups, Institute for Priestly Formation (IPF), and language immersion programs. In several cases, I found that there had never been serious academic discussion of the programs and their effect on seminary formation. These first two chapters continue the development of the problem and goal, which I have already presented in this introductory chapter, and also reveal the results of the "induction" process of van der Ven's second step. In Chapter 3, I will discuss the empirical research that I conducted, seeking information about the connection between using these programs and perseverance in ministry. This chapter presents van der Ven's third and fourth stages. The concluding chapter offers the evaluation which rounds out this Dutch theologian's approach.

Why is this study relevant?

Seminary studies in the US are not cheap. The catalogue of one seminary in the United States indicates the total direct cost to a sending diocese for seminarians in theology was just over $39,000 per year in 2019 (St. Vincent de Paul Regional Seminary, 2019, p. 44). The Association of Theological Schools, the accrediting agency for schools of theology in the United States, presents in its annual data report the average expenditure of funds per student for Roman Catholic and Protestant institutions. For 2014–2015, their estimate for Catholic graduate theological seminarians in the U.S. was just over $58,000 (Association of Theological Schools, 2016).

Seminary formation represents a significant financial cost for Catholic dioceses. Given also the time invested by seminarians in these various programmes—time that they and their bishops could look at as being taken from their time in ordained ministry—it is reasonable to ask about these programmes' effectiveness in promoting what is perhaps the most evident "product" of seminaries, priests who remain in active ministry. An example of this dynamic and the need to provide a justification for formation activities is reported by Schuth (1999, p. 204; 2002, p.143), who found that several seminaries had sought to implement the pastoral year as a requirement but faced resistance from bishops, precisely because they wanted to have the seminarians ordained as priests more quickly.

An important caveat that should be offered at this stage is that remaining in active ministry does not guarantee that a priest will serve the people well. Although it is beyond the scope of this research to determine the specific effect on the quality of priests' ministry of each of the programmes to be studied, this study offers indications as to which would be the most helpful questions to ask in this regard in further studies and which programmes would assist in promoting effective priestly ministry.

In his article, "Research on Catholic priests in the United States, since the Council: modelling the dialogue between theology and social sciencc," Bryan Froehle (2011, pp. 22–30) looked at a significant number of studies of vocations and of enrolment in seminaries, including perseverance in seminary. He mentioned no studies that specifically considered the relationship between participating in particular seminary programs and perseverance in ministry after ordination (Froehle, 2011, pp. 22–30). Furthermore, Froehle (2011, pp. 32–37) reviews a wide assortment of research into the lives of priests, some focusing on priestly morale, pastor-parochial vicar relationships, bishop-priest relationships, celibacy, alcoholism, and sexual abuse. None of the research specifically mentions any aspect of seminary formation as having an impact on perseverance or lack of perseverance in ministry.

Perhaps as relevant as the dearth of evidence on how effective these programs are at ensuring that priests remain in active long-term ministry is the question of whether there has been serious reflection on the theological and pastoral rationale for implementing them. Of the programmes being considered in the present study, Clinical Pastoral Education (CPE) has been in use by Catholic seminaries since the late 1960s (Thomas, 2006, p. 33). In his doctoral dissertation at Princeton Theological Seminary, McCarron (1981) studied the factors that led to Catholic participation in CPE. His contention, supported by a research survey that included questionnaires sent to all U.S. Catholic seminaries that were members of the Association for Clinical Pastoral Education (ACPE) at the time of his study, was that seminaries began requiring CPE not for educational or theological reasons, but to achieve purely practical goals: "The relative absence of a theological rationale and the shallowness of the educational rationale suggest that another rationale, namely, pragmatism, was a more important motive for CPE involvement by Roman Catholic seminaries" (McCarron, 1981, p.159). McCarron's work, 35 years ago, offers one example of a lacuna in research for this study to address.

What did the study try to accomplish?

The question I tried to answer in my doctoral research was: "What impact do the formation activities of Catholic seminarians have on their subsequent perseverance in ministry as ordained diocesan priests in the United States, and what specific changes in the choice of formation activities could increase the likelihood of lifelong perseverance?" I invite you to consider with me why perseverance in ministry matters and what are the theological and pastoral benefits of each of the programs included in the study?

Perhaps a spoiler alert is in order. I had hoped to be able to get enough responses to a survey of priests in and out of ministry ten years after ordination to be able to make statistically significant assessments about the relationship between participation in these programs and perseverance in ministry. The response to the survey, particularly among those who had left ministry, was too low to permit such an evaluation. The data I did garner does, however, give very helpful information about which of these programs have been most helpful for the priests who have remained in ministry for over a decade.

Chapter 1

Perseverance in Ministry: Why Does It Matter?[1]

What is perseverance?

How many times have you heard the expression: "Once a priest, always a priest"? We often talk about faithfulness and perseverance, during formation, but why? When I began my doctoral research through North-West University in South Africa, in association with the Greenwich School of Theology in England, I wanted to look at what kinds of programs seminaries and dioceses have seminarians take part in, looking at what impact, if any, they have on

[1] This chapter was originally prepared as an address at the Opening Academic Exercises at St. Vincent de Paul Regional Seminary in Boynton Beach, Florida, on August 26, 2019.

perseverance in ministry. But the research I wanted to do begged a question: Why does perseverance in ministry matter? It did not make sense to put a lot of effort into a study of the impact of programs on perseverance, if I could not show that ordained ministry is meant to be permanent. Thus, the first main part of my study, which I summarize in this chapter, addressed this question, looking at the New Testament, the Fathers, and the Magisterium: why does perseverance matter?

A caveat: the perseverance I am describing implies priesthood lived well. I will not in this presentation discuss in any detail the ways in which priesthood has not been lived well, in the distant or more recent past. I want to look at the meaning and the power of perseverance, in the hopes that we can recommit to working so that all of us who have already made a permanent commitment and all who are preparing to make it at ordination, to the diaconate and priesthood, may be joyful and effective in ministry, for the whole of our lives, of their lives.

New Testament

What does the New Testament tell us about perseverance in ministry? Even though the New Testament does not go into detail about the way that ordained ministry will be exercised in the Church, we are given some clues. Considering the powerful challenge to presbyters in 1 Peter 5:1–4 ("Tend the flock of God in your midst, [overseeing] not by constraint but willingly, as God would have it, not for shameful profit but eagerly. Do not lord it over those assigned to you, but be examples to the flock"), O'Collins and Jones (2010) maintain that Jesus "was/is the Shepherd-Priest, the Good Shepherd who was/is the Good Priest" (p. 16). We see here the golden thread throughout the tradition. Perseverance matters because it matters to the People of God. St. Peter says to the presbyters: "Be examples to the flock." As J.H. Elliott (2001) writes about this exhortation: "The Petrine instruction thus relativizes and limits the authority of elders/leaders. A domineering mode of leadership can be avoided only when leaders practice what they preach or, as is said today, when they not only 'talk the talk' but 'walk the walk'" (p. 833).

In one of his many writings on the Letter to the Hebrews, Cardinal Albert Vanhoye (2009) considers the extent to which ordained ministers share the authority of Jesus when he compares Jesus' authority "over" the People of God with Hebrews 13:17: "Obey your leaders and *defer* (Vanhoye translates in Italian with the equivalent of "submit") to them, for they keep watch over you and will have to give an account" (pp. 37–38). The authority of the ministerial priest participates in the authority of Jesus, so that he can care for the sheep and "give an account." Again, we see hints in the New Testament of the responsibility of ordained ministers to be faithful, for the sake of the faithful, for whom they have to render an account.

In the Pastoral Letters, especially in 2 Timothy, we see indications of what the ordained minister needs to do to strengthen himself for ministry and why. In 2 Timothy 1:6, Paul calls Timothy to "stir into flame the gift of God that you have through the imposition of my hands." Luke Timothy Johnson (2001) translates this verse: "I remind you to revivify that special gift for service that God gave you through the laying on of my hands" (pp. 344–345). The very intense challenge Paul gives to Timothy here (Johnson argues for authentic Pauline authorship) can be applied to ordained ministers in the Church today. The power received at ordination is not given by the Bishop or by the institutional Church, it is given by God (cf. Johnson, 2001, p. 354). As the next verse says, "God did not give us a spirit of cowardice but rather of power and love and self-control" (2 Tm 1:7). The challenges of ministry and of martyrdom, addressed throughout this letter, are all possible to meet if Timothy "stirs into flame" or "revivifies" the gifts received by the laying on of hands. In discussing the permanence of priestly ministry, in a context where very often it can seem that the joy of the first days of ministry do not last for long, the charge to Timothy to remember the first days of faith and ministry and bring the gifts once received back to life, like someone bringing a smoldering fire back into flame, is a helpful image. It is good to remember that Timothy is told that he was given this gift for a purpose, "for service."

The second chapter of the Second Letter to Timothy offers specific examples for imitation to share efficaciously in the sufferings of Christ. The willingness to suffer, like Paul, whether in imitation of a soldier or an athlete or a farmer, is essential for success in ministry (Johnson, 2001, p. 371). This point resonates with the concern for perseverance in ministry. And this willingness to suffer is not an abstract matter, but is linked specifically to the good of the people being served: "I bear with everything for the sake of those who are chosen, so that they too may obtain the salvation that is in Christ Jesus, together with eternal glory" (2 Tm 2:10). Paul is encouraging Timothy to be faithful, in imitation of himself and, in the end, of Jesus, precisely because we can rely that we will share the resurrection if we share the cross (cf. 2 Tm 2:11). Johnson's (2011) translation and interpretation of this verse gives it a particular meaning, in that he renders *pistos ho logos* as "the word of God is faithful" (p. 381), not just that the saying that follows is trustworthy. To see the presbyter's call to faithfulness, even and especially in the midst of suffering, as an expression of his commitment to the good of the people he serves and of his reliance on the faithfulness of God, offers a positive contribution to the discussion of the meaning of priestly perseverance.

The Fathers

Of the early Church Fathers, St. Clement of Rome (ca. 97, 1994) is an important witness to the permanence of ordained ministry, with his opposition to the removal from ministry of leaders of the community: "For our sin will not be small, if we eject from the episcopate those who have blamelessly and holily performed its duties [presented the offerings]" (p. 17). St. Ignatius of Antioch, with his sense of the importance of the three-fold ministry of bishops, presbyters, and deacons for the unity of the Church, indicates indirectly why their perseverance matters, since "apart from these, there is no Church" (Ignatius of Antioch, ca. 107, 1994, p. 67).

Before Nicaea, St. Irenaeus of Lyons writes about the importance of obeying good and faithful ministers and avoiding the unfaithful. While he does not address the question of whether unfaithful presbyters remain as presbyters — a question that would later be addressed by Augustine — Irenaeus (bet. 182–188, 1994) speaks powerfully of both the authority and responsibility of the presbyter as teacher and promoter of unity (pp. 497–498). By the early third century, "all ministry is seen consistently as a call and commission from the Lord. Nowhere is there mention of self-appointment or even community appointment to ministry" (Osborne, 1988, p.128). This point affirms the importance of perseverance in ministry since it is God's call, not the choice of the community or the minister himself.

Of the great Fathers of the Church, from the West, we need to consider St. Augustine. He prepares the way for the later teaching on the sacramental character in his discussion of the validity of baptism by heretics. Augustine (ca. 400, 1994a) presents "the analogy of the military mark, which, though it can both be retained as by deserters, and, also be received by those who are not in the army, yet ought not to be either received or retained outside its ranks; and, at the same time, it is not changed or renewed when a man is enlisted or brought back to his service" (p. 414). The clear teaching is that someone who has been baptized and, by analogy, ordained, cannot receive this sacrament again.

Augustine also uses the permanence of ordination, which he assumes as a given, as a support for his teaching on the permanence of marriage. Augustine's argument is that ordination indeed takes place for the good of the Christian people, but this good supposes that ordination imparts a permanent change. The very comparison with marriage leads to the conclusion that this permanent mark given to the ordained presbyter is a relational seal: the man is set in a permanent relationship with the People of God, for the good of the members of the Church. It may be a fruitful relationship or not (he recognizes that the people may or not follow him), and he may be faithful or not (there is a possibility of removal from office), but the priest and the bishop — like the husband who may or may not have children or who may or may not be faithful — is forever marked by his ordination. Augustine (ca. 401, 1994b) does not get into the specific difference between the cases, relating to the possibility of marriage after the death of a spouse and the ontological nature that later theology will apply to the character of orders, but the comparison is enlightening (p. 412).

From the East, we need to consider St. John Chrysostom. While Chrysostom (ca. 377, 1994) writes eloquently of the dignity of the priesthood, he does so not as one who is looking for glory (pp. 48–50). He instead fears the responsibility of the priest for the good of the Christian people as he expresses his unworthiness ordination. Citing 1 Timothy 3:1, he opines, "I have not said that it is a terrible thing to desire the work, but only the authority and power" (John Chrysostom, ca. 377, 1994, p. 50). As he expressed reasons for being afraid of the episcopal/priestly office, Chrysostom could be said to describe the qualities needed in a priest: "sober-minded and penetrating in discernment" (Chrysostom, ca. 377, 1994, p. 51), avoidance of anger, "perpetual watchfulness concerning his manner of life, lest someone discovering an exposed and neglected spot should inflict a deadly wound," and ability to resist many temptations against humility (Chrysostom c. 377, 1994, p. 52). He goes on to summarize the needed gifts of the priest: "he ought to be dignified yet free from arrogance, formidable yet kind, apt to command yet sociable, impartial yet courteous, humble yet not servile, strong yet gentle" (Chrysostom, ca. 377, 1994, p. 55). These qualities are reminiscent of the elements of a modern program of formation, at least of human and pastoral formation, which should prepare all future priests (and current priests) for "perpetual watchfulness concerning his manner of life."

The Scholastics

As we fast-forward to the era of Scholastic theology, then-Monsignor David Toups (2004) summarizes the thought of St. Thomas Aquinas about the sacramental character, as the permanent mark of ordination (and the other sacraments which cannot be repeated) comes to be called, and indicates why it is relevant today: "This character is a spiritual power which deputes the minister to make present the mysteries of Christ in Christian worship.... To the priest, it is a reminder of his permanent relationship with Christ the High Priest. The sacramental character makes the priest's sacramental ministry a gift to the Church" (p. 142). The indelible mark guarantees the priest's sacramental ministry regardless of his own worthiness (Toups, 2004, p. 142). Once again, although the theological language concentrates on what happens to the priest, it also upholds the good of the Christian people. The people benefit from the theology of character, insofar as it guarantees the validity of the sacraments in which they take part.

Protestant Reformation

A brief glance at the thought of Martin Luther helps us to see how much negative impact the bad example of corrupt clergy can have, leading this Reformer to turn upside down the entire tradition supporting permanence in ministry. Luther (1523) argued for the removal from Bohemia of priests faithful to the pope, even preferring for Christians to go without the Eucharist if that be the price: "For the Eucharist is not so necessary that salvation depends on it. The gospel and baptism are sufficient, since faith alone justifies and love alone lives rightly" (p. 9). This argument goes against the entire tradition, that defended the validity of a priest's acts motivated by the good of the people and their right to the sacraments.

Trent

The Council of Trent, then, had to defend the tradition about permanence in ministry, specifically addressing priestly character. Among the canons of the Council of Trent, the one most clearly related to this issue is canon 4 from Session 23: "If anyone says that by sacred ordination the Holy Spirit is not given and that, therefore, the bishops say in vain: 'Receive the Holy Spirit'; or if he says that no character is imprinted by ordination; or that he who has once been a priest can again become a layman, let him be anathema" (Hünermann, 2012, p. 424, §1774). The logic for Trent's insistence on the permanence and effectiveness of ordination, according to Osborne (1988), is christological and eucharistic: "If the ordination ritual, with its injunction to priests to offer sacrifice, is interpreted in a way which diminishes the complete efficacy of the work of Jesus, then an invocation of the Holy Spirit is, indeed, an unworthy prayer" (p. 267). It is because the Holy Spirit's invocation is effective that the priest can offer sacrifice and that he remains a priest forever. To deny the reliability of the Holy Spirit: what could cause greater harm to the People of God? Trent may not have put it in those terms, but the theme we have been proposing, that perseverance in ministry matters because it matters to the People of God, is seen again.

Pope Pius XI

Coming now to the last century, Pope Pius XI is often perceived today as highly conservative, but prepared the way for the theological growth that would follow. Pius XI specifically links the permanence of priesthood not just with his sacramental power, but also with his responsibility to the Church:

> These august powers are conferred upon the priest in a special Sacrament designed to this end: they are not merely passing or temporary in the priest, but are stable and perpetual, united as they are with the indelible character imprinted on his soul whereby he becomes "a priest forever"; whereby he becomes like unto Him in whose eternal priesthood he has been made a sharer. Even the most lamentable downfall, which, through human frailty, is possible to a priest, can

> never blot out from his soul the priestly character. But along with this character and these powers, the priest through the Sacrament of Orders receives new and special grace with special helps. Thereby, if only he will loyally further, by his free and personal cooperation, the divinely powerful action of the grace itself, he will be able worthily to fulfil all the duties, however arduous, of his lofty calling. He will not be overborne, but will be able to bear the tremendous responsibilities inherent to his priestly duty; responsibilities which have made fearful even the stoutest champions of the Christian priesthood, men like St. John Chrysostom, St. Ambrose, St. Gregory the Great, St. Charles and many others (Pius XI, 1935, §22).

Pius XI was very clear about the importance of making sure that men were prepared well for the priesthood and that if they were in the seminary for the wrong reasons or if their vocation was not well-tested, they should not be ordained. He wanted to protect the Church (not just the institution, but what Vatican II would later call the People of God), and thus he wrote to Bishops (and indirectly to seminary formators): "do not fear to seem harsh if, in virtue of your rights and fulfilling your duty, you require such positive proofs of worthiness before ordination; or if you defer an ordination in case of doubt" (Pius XI, 1935, §73). For Pius XI, priesthood is definitely a permanent state, but he saw how urgent it is to be sure that a man is well-prepared for the commitment before making it. We want a man to be a priest forever, but Bishops need to refrain from ordaining those who are not worthy of or able to fulfill this commitment!

Vatican II

The Second Vatican Council certainly deepened the Church's reflection on the priesthood, especially regarding the relationship between the priesthood of the faithful and that of ordained ministers. Cardinal Avery Dulles (1997) speaks of the priest's service to the community in discussing *Lumen Gentium* 10, which describes the difference between these two ways of sharing in the priesthood of Jesus Christ as being of "essence" and not "degree":

> The council refuses to attribute a higher grade or degree to the ministerial, as though the common priesthood ranked lower than it on the same scale. Instead, it situates the two kinds of priesthood in different categories, like oranges and apples. The ministerial priesthood involves a public representational function rather than a personal giftedness. If anything, the common priesthood is more exalted, for the ministers are ordained for the sake of service toward the whole people of God (p. 11).

The notion of permanence and excellence in ministry is also affirmed by *Presbyterorum Ordinis*:

> Hence, this holy council, to fulfil its pastoral desires of an internal renewal of the Church, of the spread of the Gospel in every land and of a dialogue with the world of today, strongly urges all priests that they strive always for that growth in holiness by which they will become consistently better instruments in the service of the whole People of God, using for this purpose those

means which the Church has approved" (Vatican II, 1965, §12).

Clearly this call to perseverance and to holiness is linked to the service priests are called to offer to the Church. The Council calls for priests to do what might be called theological reflection with regard to all of their tasks in ministry, something that should certainly be learned in seminary formation: "In order to measure and verify this coordination of life in a concrete way, let priests examine all their works and projects to see what is the will of God — namely, to see how their endeavors compare with the goals of the Gospel mission of the Church" (Vatican II, 1965, §14). A challenge for us in formation and a challenge for all priests is to continually examine ourselves, to seek to be united each day more fully to the will of God so that we can live out our vocation more fully and more completely. Aware that priests have received a special character at ordination, which conforms us, in the words of the Council, to the person of *Christi capitis*, "Christ the Head," the question becomes how we give ourselves more fully each day to the Body of Christ, who is also, following the imagery of Ephesians 5, also our Bride. The language of the nuptial relationship of the priest to the Church and that of the priest as father (precisely because he is Bridegroom) assists us in looking at perseverance, once again from the perspective of the relationship between the priest and his people.

The Council Fathers, in the conclusion to *Presbyterorum Ordinis*, recalled the challenges facing priests and encouraged them to trust in God and support each other: "Having before our eyes the joys of the priestly life, this holy synod cannot at the same time overlook the difficulties which priests experience in the circumstances of contemporary life" (Vatican II, 1965, §22). Over 50 years ago, Vatican II saw the challenges that faced priests and faithful living in a world where they would have to be countercultural. In formation for the priesthood, seminaries need to continue to prepare seminarians for these challenges, always present and yet always new.

Post-Conciliar Theology

There has certainly been much development in

the theology of priesthood in the last five and a half decades since the close of the Vatican Council. To conclude this discussion, though, I will only consider a couple of additional comments about how the perseverance of ministers of her priests impacts the life of the Church. In his dissertation on the importance of sacramental character, then-Msgr. Toups comments on the dangers of functionalism in the life of a priest: "Balance is needed in the life of the priest: the priestly life is about being and doing. It appears that those who have left failed to make a 'presumption for perseverance and permanence' which is the proper response to the sacerdotal character received at ordination" (Toups, 2004, p. 51). One danger is that some priests may affirm the value of permanence in ministry but focus so much on what they do that they lose sight of who they are. To avoid functionalism, strengthening a sense of identity and promoting the value of perseverance are key (Toups, 2004, p. 91).

Richard Gaillardetz (2003) argues that, rather than abandoning (as many do) the ontological notion that underlies the discussion of the permanent character associated with baptism, confirmation, and holy orders, the task for today is to "shift to a 'relational ontology' in which attention is drawn not to the isolated individual, but to the person-in-relation" (p. 40). Affirming the ontological effects on the person in ordination (as well as baptism and confirmation), he writes that "any such 'ontological change' is grounded not in the conferral of powers on an individual but on the reconfiguration of the person into a new ecclesial relation" (Gaillardetz, 2003, p. 40).

These comments, from theologians who approach priesthood and formation from different angles, both focus on the priest as one who is in relationship, with Christ and the Church. That relationship is permanent, precisely for the good of the People of God. Without entering into detail of the many Church documents and the reflections of other theologians since the Council, this expression of the *Ratio Fundamentalis* (Congregation for the Clergy 2016) puts the priest's conformation to Christ in the context of the absolute nature of Christ's self-giving on behalf of humanity: "The priest is therefore called to form himself so that his heart and his life are conformed to the Lord Jesus, in this way becoming a sign of the love God has for each person" (p. 21).

Perseverance for the sake of the People of God

Seeing perseverance considering the priest's relationship with the People of God and his love for them has particular resonance, we have seen, in the image of priest as Bridegroom. It holds as well with the image of the priest as father, as presented in Father Carter Griffin's recent work (2019). A concluding anecdote may put the importance of perseverance in context, at a moment when all commitments can seem cheap and impermanent, and when a kind of spiritual and existential FOMO ("fear of missing out") can keep us always looking for other options. Learning of a priest who had "discerned" that he was being called to the married life (I cannot get past that clause without noting that it is an abuse of Ignatian discernment to mention in the same breath discernment and breaking the permanent commitments of marriage, ordination, or religious life [Zollner, 2005]), a friend, married with children, asked me: "How can that be? Can I 'discern' that I don't have to be faithful to my wife? That I don't have to care for my children?" In the end, over 2,000 years of Christian history, many theological supports have been offered for the understanding that priesthood is forever. Perseverance matters most because we need to be faithful to our Bride and our children. The People of God need our faithfulness.

Chapter 2

A Study of Seminary Formation Programs

What programs?

In my doctoral research I sought to investigate the impact on perseverance in ministry of participation in some of the formation activities that might be considered optional for seminaries, dioceses, or for seminarians themselves. The programs I examined were Clinical Pastoral Education (CPE), spirituality or propaedeutic year, pastoral-year internships, priestly-fraternity groups (such as Emmaus or Jesus Caritas), the Institute of Priestly Formation (IPF), and language immersion programs. An important step in the process was to look at each of these programs, in terms of its history and structure, its theological rationale, and its practical purpose. One of my most immediate findings was that there was very little written about most of them. Given the importance these programs can have in the formation of seminarians, in this article, in the present chapter, we will see some of the highlights of the study of each of these programs, leading to theological reflection on the use of these formation activity in seminary formation, especially in terms of their potential impact on preparing seminarians for a permanent commitment to priestly ministry.

Clinical Pastoral Education (CPE)

Clinical Pastoral Education (CPE) is a formation activity for ministers, with its roots in the work of Anton Boisen (R. Powell, 2005, p. 317). Boisen established the first hospital-based training program for Protestant seminary students in 1924, and he wanted to get support from seminary administrators, to require "a year of required clinical experience as the means of revitalizing their entire academic programs" (Powell, 2005:17).

Hemenway (2005, p. 23) offers a definition for

CPE:

> ... an educational methodology that combines knowledge of psychology (who we are) with knowledge of theology (what we believe) with process education (how we learn) in order to prepare seminarians, clergy, and qualified lay people to provide effective interfaith spiritual care among the religious and social complexities of the modern world.

Some of the elements of CPE training include weekly didactic sessions and the presentation of cases by students; small groups meet to process the experiences once or twice per week (Hemenway, 2005, p. 23). Hemenway (2005) describes the model as "action-reflection" (p. 23). The purpose of the small group experience is not only to help students to develop their clinical skills, but also "to understand organizational and systems dynamics in an increasingly complex world" (Hemenway, 2005, p. 23). CPE emphasizes forming ministers who can work in interfaith and cross-cultural situations (Hemenway, 2005, p. 332).

Since the 1960s, CPE programs have been common in Catholic seminaries. Sister Katerina Schuth (2016) reports that CPE, a program that was once required by almost all Catholic seminaries in the United States, has declined in popularity among these institutions (pp. 113, 175). Nine seminaries (out of 39 US theological seminaries) required a summer CPE experience as of 2016, and seven others offered it as an elective option (Schuth, 2016, pp. 113, 175). As recently as 2000, 24 seminaries required CPE for all seminarians in theology; since then the CPE requirement has often been replaced by other hospital ministry programs (Schuth, 2016, pp. 31, 113).

One example of a replacement program that seeks to provide a Catholic formation context to formation in hospital ministry is the Spiritual Pastoral Ministry summer experience at St. Paul Seminary in Minnesota. The manual for the program describes its purpose, as it relates to the healthcare aspects:

> The goal of this program is to help seminarians grow in their ministerial identity so as to become

> instruments of God's healing in ministry to the sick and suffering. The seminarian develops pastoral skills in visiting the sick, integrating theological concepts with ministry and developing listening skills, viewed from a Catholic theological and formational perspective (St. Paul Seminary School of Divinity, Department of Pastoral Formation, 2013, p. 7).

Another seminary offers a choice between CPE and a summer hospital immersion program under the supervision of its pastoral department; those in charge of pastoral formation at this seminary report that they find increased maturity in participants after CPE (Clarke, 2011a, p. 34).

One concern expressed about CPE programs is the uneven formation of supervisors. In their 2009 study of the training of CPE supervisors, Ragsdale *et al.* (2009) found only three studies in 20 years that had attempted to study the preparation of these professionals who play a key role in the preparation of ministers: "At this point ACPE (Association for Clinical Pastoral Education) lacks any kind of formal holding environment to help CPE supervisors doing supervisory education reflect on their own process of self-awareness, supervisory skill development, theoretical development, and on-going integration" (pp. 1, 13).

According to Little (2010), the "action/reflection method" used by CPE "is excellent for understanding the pastoral interaction but does not necessarily facilitate the further development of the propositional knowledge base" (p. 11). He argues that much of the information shared during group supervision sessions comes from the experiences of the participants themselves, so how much other participants learn depends on presenting participants' knowledge and depth of reflection. There can be the danger, as I remember hearing my first Pastor describing youth group faith sharing, of "shared ignorance."

The validity of evaluations written by CPE supervisors is also a matter of concern: "These evaluations reflect the values of the supervisor and are not standard across supervisors or the various centers. Lacking standardization, there is no professionally acceptable common standard of competence" (Little, 2010, p. 6.) The *PPF,* 5th Edition (USCCB, 2006) specifically mandates that supervisors receive proper formation: "Onsite supervisors should be carefully selected with an eye to their dedication to the Church and respect for the priesthood. They should be taught the skills of pastoral supervision and evaluation" (p. 86).

The *PPF* (USCCB, 2006) also calls for formation programs not based in a seminary setting to be vetted, to ensure that they support formation to the Catholic priesthood:

> Seminaries and dioceses that make provision for onsite experiences are also responsible for ensuring that these experiences help seminarians develop skills and attitudes that will enhance their future priestly ministry and that, when ecumenical in nature, for example, CPE, are respectful of the Catholic teaching, especially on moral or ethical issues. It is the responsibility of the diocesan bishop, religious ordinary, and the rectors to ensure that the Catholic, sacramental dimension of pastoral care is integral to all such programs in which seminarians participate (p. 83).

The first study I found of the participation of Catholic seminarians in CPE was a doctoral dissertation at Princeton Theological Seminary by Father Gerald J. McCarron in 1981. He studied the factors that led to Catholic participation in CPE. After conducting a study that included sending questionnaires to all US Catholic seminaries that were then members of the Association for Clinical Pastoral Education (ACPE), he concluded that the reasons for the use of CPE were not truly educational and certainly not theological, but primarily pragmatic: "The relative absence of a theological rationale and the shallowness of the educational rationale suggest that another rationale, namely, pragmatism, was a more important motive for CPE involvement by Roman Catholic seminaries" (McCarron, 1981, p. 159.) Relying on the thinking of W. James and F.C.S. Schiller, McCarron (1981) defines pragmatism as "If something works do it," and he comments:

> To a great extent the kind of pragmatism that I am talking about has to be described in negative terms. It is described in terms of what it lacks —

> a theoretical basis and the use of given means in a manner that is more than expedient. In a more positive vein pragmatism can also be viewed as one of the strengths of American Roman Catholicism. It indicates a willingness to innovate and to take risks even when it is not completely clear what the results will be (McCarron, 1981, pp. 160, 162–163).

McCarron (1981:169) mentioned a variety of ways that there could be deeper reflection on the Catholic seminaries' purposes for using CPE. He asked a question still relevant almost four decades later: "How will 'Catholic issues' — celibacy, sacramentality, particularly the sacramentality of the priesthood — be integrated into CPE programs?"[2] The vision of priests as not only celebrating the sacraments, but also of being representatives of Christ, is

---

[2] The sacramentality of the priesthood is expressed in *Presbyterorum ordinis* 1: "Wherefore the priesthood, while indeed it presupposes the sacraments of Christian initiation, is conferred by that special sacrament; through it priests, by the anointing of the Holy Spirit, are signed with a special character and are conformed to Christ the Priest in such a way that they can act in the person of Christ the Head."

at stake here.

One seminary describes CPE in this way, which reflects the way many of us in seminary formation have approached CPE:

> Clinical Pastoral Education (CPE) is a proven program for developing the important skills for working with the sick, the hospitalized, and the grieving. Additionally, it offers the seminarian a focused, supervised opportunity for introspection and theological reflection; it is therefore highly recommended for all theology students. Seminarians usually complete one basic unit of CPE after the second or third year of theology (Mount Angel Seminary, 2015, p. 45).

Although this catalog describes CPE as a "proven program," an indication of the paucity of information about the effectiveness, by any measure, of CPE for Catholic seminarians, can be found in the results of a web search using the terms *Catholic, seminarian, CPE.* In such a search in early 2017, eight of the first ten choices were articles or blogs highly critical of the CPE experience for Catholic seminarians (Google, 2017).

Father Philip Neri Powell (2009), a Dominican priest currently on the faculty of a large seminary in the US, describes his experience in CPE in the early 2000s on his blog:

> Clinical Pastoral Education is nothing more than a systematic 'weeding out' of orthodox seminarians through a process of enforced radical leftist indoctrination. I survived [because] I was 37 years old and had years of working in mental health institutions under my belt. I was able to manipulate the system using the rhetoric and strategy of victimization that seemed to garner the attention of the administration.

He offers advice to seminarians entering CPE programs, advice that assumes the CPE experience will be negative:

> Can you learn something from CPE? You better believe it! I did. But I learned in spite of [what] passed for Catholic pastoral care at [the hospital where he participated in CPE]. I learned from the

> patients and their families. I learned from the nurses and doctors. I also learned from the chaplains.... I learned exactly how NOT to be a Catholic minister (Powell, 2009).

Most of the posts on this blog are negative towards CPE, and Powell (2009) later added a comment: "I still maintain that our American bishops need to re-evaluate and reform the CPE process for Catholic seminarians so that the unique character of the priestly charism is honored and developed." He goes on to explain:

> Though CPE programs have tempered their more abusive practices in recent years, the focus is still too narrowly placed on the therapeutic restructuring of the student's fundamental belief system to accord with mainstream-liberal Protestant norms for [what] counts as ministry to the sick. [In other words], too often Catholic seminarians are pressured to hold and practice an essentially anti-sacramental view of ministry to the sick and dying (Powell, 2009).

Ordination relates the presbyter both to God and to the People of God, two relationships that give the permanence of priesthood its theological foundation and thus explain why presbyters ought to persevere in ministry. The material available about CPE programs suggests that they could be of service in helping a seminarian know himself better and thus be better able to give himself fully in priesthood. At the same time, Catholic seminarians and priests who participated in CPE have expressed serious concerns about the experience. While these remarks are anecdotal in nature, they reflect the concern that had already been raised in the *PPF*, 5th Edition (USCCB, 2006:83):

> Seminaries and dioceses that make provision for onsite experiences are also responsible for ensuring that these experiences help seminarians develop skills and attitudes that will enhance their future priestly ministry and that, when ecumenical in nature, for example, CPE, are respectful of the Catholic teaching, especially on moral or ethical issues.

As G. Ferraro (2006, p. 777–787) suggested, the Holy Spirit is always making a priest's whole life the fruit of an epiclesis. A useful question would ask whether it would be possible for seminaries that wish their seminarians to take part in CPE programs, without compromising the integrity of these programs, to collaborate more with them to ensure that the Catholic understanding of sacramental ministry and the role of the Holy Spirit will be respected. Unless supervisors recognize that the Holy Spirit is the primary actor in the ministerial life of the future priest, pastoral experiences will fail to promote a clear sense of ministerial identity as rooted in baptism but destined to blossom in a permanent commitment to priestly service.

Spirituality or propaedeutic year

The Congregation for the Clergy's 2016 *Ratio Fundamentalis* has changed the discussion regarding this second formation activity to be considered. The Congregation for the Clergy (2016) describes what it calls the "propaedeutic stage": "Its principal objective is to provide a solid basis for the spiritual life and to mature a greater self-awareness for personal growth" (p. 28). After listing some of the activities that should mark this experience, the *Ratio* (2016) indicates that each national conference can adapt this stage, depending on the reality of the Church in a particular country and diocese (Congregation for the Clergy, p. 29).

Even before this Vatican document, Hoge (2006), because of his extensive research on recently ordained priests, specifically recommended an improvement in spiritual formation (p. 6). Furthermore, Rossetti (2011) concludes his book, *Why priests are happy*, with a series of recommendations, including this one: "During the formative years, work intensely with seminarians on their spiritual formation, fostering a direct, personal relationship with God." His study indicates that the spiritual life is central to the happiness and success of the priest, and formation for this life must begin in seminary (p. 195). The spirituality year or propaedeutic year, as it has been conceived until now, as well as the Institute for Priestly Formation, to be examined below, aim for the fostering of the "direct, personal relationship with God," as a precondition for the rest of seminary formation and for effective priestly ministry.

Only two seminaries in the United States have intentionally adopted programs which aim to fulfil what the Holy See describes as a propaedeutic stage, using the term "spirituality year," although these activities treat subjects in addition to spirituality. Some of the recommendations and concerns revealed in extensive research of recently ordained priests, according to Schuth (2002), included a need for deeper prayer life in seminary (p. 142). In response to such concerns, the *Spiritual Year Formation Booklet* (St. John Vianney Theological Seminary, 2016) indicates that its purpose is to afford seminarians the opportunity to strengthen their spiritual life by giving an entire year to this effort (p. 4). In describing the rationale for the Spirituality Year at the Denver seminary, Father James Thermos (2017) cites the call of *Pastores Dabo Vobis* (John Paul II, 1992) for significant preparation before priesthood candidates enter seminary. In making this call, St. John Paul II asked for a period of experimentation, to which these programs being considered seek to respond. John Paul II did not attempt to say exactly what form this preparation should take:

> While there is increasing consensus regarding the need for preparation prior to the major seminary, there are different ideas as to what such preparation should contain and what its characteristics should be: Should it be directed mainly to spiritual formation to discern the vocation or to intellectual and cultural formation? (§62).

The horarium for the spirituality year at St. Charles Borromeo in Philadelphia includes prayer several times during the day, study of topics including the Bible, the basics of the Catholic faith and spiritual texts from the tradition, as well as conferences on topics important to priesthood and ministry. Seminarians are required to go on a "media fast — no cell phones, TV, computers." They also devote time for work in their common house as well as sports and exercise (Ravitz, p. 2015).

At St. John Vianney Theological Seminary in Denver, Colorado, the spirituality year follows a similar schedule. As at St. Charles Borromeo, seminarians observe a media fast six days a week, excluding Saturdays. Seminarians go to local parishes on Sundays to assist in pastoral work and watch a movie together in the evening from a selected group of inspirational films (St. John Vianney Theological Seminary, 2016, pp. 16–17).

Other attempts have been made to ensure the preparation of candidates for seminary. Some of the same intentions can be found in other programs, which may not require a full year before entering the regular seminary program but call for extensive periods of spiritual focus. St. John Seminary in Camarillo requires several intense experiences on the seminary grounds (Clarke, 2011b, pp. 32–33). There are two four-week intensive spiritual formation activities over two summers "similar to a diocesan novitiate, focusing on prayer, spirituality, silent retreat and reflection on personal issues for greater self-understanding and healing" (Clarke, 2011b, p. 33)

These two summers of intensive spiritual experiences, before II Theology and before III Theology (after the pastoral year internship), seek, during the first experience, to link spiritual formation with human formation, and in the second, to link spiritual formation with pastoral formation (Clarke, 2011a, pp. 30–31). The purpose is "a greater integration and understanding of the connectedness and health of their body, mind, and spirit in ministry" (Clarke, 2011a, p 31). Although this seminary does not currently have a spirituality or propaedeutic year, the aims of the Camarillo program are similar to those of the propaedeutic or spirituality year model.

What are such programs trying to accomplish? Father James Rafferty (2011) touches on the need that they are trying to address: the importance of seminarians' experiencing true communion with Christ before asking to be ordained to act in the name of Christ. He writes: "All the components of spiritual formation promote the seminarian's falling deeper in love with the Trinity, because he opens himself in daily prayer to receive the infinite love of God for him uniquely" (Rafferty, p. 36.)

In writing about the role of seminaries in continuing formation activities for priests, Camelli (2008) discusses the importance of perseverance in ministry. He writes with concern about priests' leaving active ministry and strongly urges seminarians to commit to pursuing ongoing formation after their ordination (p. 17). Programs such as a spirituality year or the pastoral year, in different ways, seek to make the link between learning and the life of seminarians and priests. A specific suggestion regarding spiritual formation is that seminaries should encourage seminarians to long for continuous spiritual growth. A desire for "a continuous conversion of heart" needs to be at the center of seminary spiritual formation (Camelli, 2008, p. 21). Promoting this desire is part of the rationale of the spirituality or propaedeutic year.

How effective are these programs in preparing men for seminary and in promoting perseverance in those who are ordained priests? Thermos (2017) indicates that they have no statistical data to report that would assist in answering this question. He writes, however:

> Consistently we observe the seminarians coming to a much greater degree of self-knowledge, self-acceptance, affective maturity, freedom, healthy image of God, greater understanding of the priestly vocation, deeper prayer life (relating in a personal way to each of the Three Persons of the

Blessed Trinity and to Our Blessed Mother), growth in moral character, embrace of poverty, chastity and obedience, understanding of the faith, love for the Church, desire to serve Christ in the poor and share in His mission. Consequently, they begin to understand and respond to the invitation presented to them in their vocational call with greater clarity, freedom and zeal (Thermos, 2017).

With regard to the impending requirement of a propaedeutic stage for all seminarians, the *Ratio fundamentalis* states, "Following the experiment-tation and trial period, begun by the Synod of Bishops of 1990 (VIII General Assembly), the 'propaedeutic stage', with its specific identity and formative purpose, is now presented as necessary and mandatory" (Congregation for the Clergy 2016, p. 5). The Congregation for the Clergy (2016) offers suggestions made as early as 1980 for this period of preparation before seminary and presents the new requirement in this way: "The experience of recent decades has revealed the need to dedicate a period of time to preparation of an introductory nature, in view of the priestly formation to follow or, alternatively, of a decision to follow a different path in life" (p. 28, n. 93). Calling for this period to last one or two years, the document goes on: "The propaedeutic stage is an indispensable phase of formation.... Its principal objective is to provide a solid base for the spiritual life and to nurture a greater self-awareness for personal growth" (Congregation for the Clergy, 2016, p. 28).

The exact design expected of such programs is not clear in the Vatican document. The Congregation for the Clergy (2016) expresses the need to establish programs that are adapted to the needs of each country, while calling for the propaedeutic stage to be distinct from the succeeding stages of seminary formation (p. 29). The very small number of seminaries currently requiring such programs in the United States makes it difficult to assess how effective they have been in preparing candidates for seminary and subsequent ministry. Part of the purpose of my doctoral research was to offer some initial data to assist in the evaluation what has been done until now and offer insight in the design of propaedeutic programs for the future.

Pastoral-year internship

The idea of an extended pastoral experience, whether before or after ordination to the diaconate, has been around since the 1960s. Before the close of Vatican II, Geany (1965) (p. 479) defined pastoral activity "not as an appendage to the priestly ministry, but as indivisible from its essence" (p. 479). A solution that was attempted at the time of the Council was to have seminarians do a fifth year in "so-called pastoral theology," the study of which the 1956 Apostolic Constitution *Sedes Sapientiae* had already required for seminarians preparing for ordination as religious priests (Geany, 1965, p. 489). Recognizing the danger of a disconnect in seminary formation between the life of the future priest and pastoral ministry, Geany writes: "Thus in a pastorally-thrusted seminary, there must exist the unified duality of scholarly theology and the living dialogue with the areas of life to be affected by and infused with this theology" (Geany, 1965, p. 489).

Bishop G. Huyghe of Arras, France, in 1964 required a diaconal year in a parish before ordination to the priesthood and invited the laity to share in the preparation of men to the priesthood in a way that would connect with their future work in parishes (Geany, 1965, p. 489). Geany (1965) argued, though, that the reflection on the bond between Gospel and action must take place not just at the end of seminary formation, but throughout the seminary experience. (p. 490).

Sister Leanne Hubbard and Sister Mary Regina Rollins (2017) describe the pastoral internship at St. John's Seminary in Camarillo, California, as a two-semester experience in a parish, taking place between the second and third years of theology. During this time, the seminarians work in parishes, under the supervision of experienced pastors, while remaining in contact with the seminary's field education staff and with other interns for online discussions of "theological reflection, homily review and administrative and pastoral case studies" (Hubbard & Rollins, 2017). These sessions not only assist in providing concrete information and formation to the seminarians, but also help them to keep their internship work in context, keeping the seminarians in communication with the seminary since they receive graduate credit for the experience and have to respond to the seminary for their performance (Hubbard & Rollins, 2017). The pastoral-year program at St. Vincent de Paul Regional Seminary in Boynton Beach, Florida, requires two week-long workshops on the seminary campus (one per semester), as well as two online courses, in which material in the courses is related to the work the interns are doing, one course in catechesis and evangelization and the other in parish administration (St. Vincent de Paul Regional Seminary, 2016, p. 22). After an extensive study of priests ordained between five and nine years, Hoge (2006) recommended that seminaries offer more opportunities for pastoral formation, specifically endorsing the pastoral year model (p. 6).

Hubbard and Rollins (2017) clearly articulate the purposes of this year: learning about pastoral ministry, deepening discernment about the call to priesthood, and discerning the seminarian's pastoral gifts. They comment further:

> (The interns) are not ordained workers but learners, observers, and ministers testing out as many aspects of parish life as possible within

> their competencies. When they return for third and fourth theology they engage the theology classes pastorally, with an eye to the real experiences from the parish. This year is also seen as a watershed discernment year. Does being immersed in the parish solidify further the priestly vocation or call it further into question? (Hubbard & Rollins, 2017).

Since discernment is done not only by seminarians, but also by those charged with their formation and with recommending them to their bishops for ordination, it is important that the seminary receive feedback that can inform that process of ecclesial discernment. Thus, evaluation is a key element of any formation activity. Hubbard and Rollins (2017) consider the importance of preparing supervisors to provide appropriate supervision and offer evaluations helpful to the formation process. They describe ways in which the evaluations of the program by the interns themselves helped to improve their program. At St. Vincent de Paul in Florida, a rubric with 21 criteria is used for pastoral-year supervisors to complete for each intern, in addition to an interim evaluation in the first semester, regular phone calls to interns and supervisors, and visits by seminary staff to each site at least once during the year (St. Vincent de Paul Regional Seminary, 2017, pp. 1–11).

The formation faculty at St. John's in Camarillo find that the pastoral-year internship is an essential part of formation. The seminary has found that seminarians "return ... with greater self-confidence; they are more grounded and secure in their vocational discernment.... As a result of their pastoral immersion experience, we notice a greater commitment to the final two years of theological studies" (Clarke, 2011b, p. 33). These areas of growth, especially vocational discernment and greater dedication to their studies after the pastoral internship, are clearly essential for the successful completion of seminary and for future success in priesthood.

An important value in field education, according to Ann Garrido (2010), is the development of "priestly identity and authority," which longer-term pastoral assignments afford the time to develop (32-33). The importance of field education for assessment is also mentioned by Garrido (2010:33–34).

Assessment is important so that the pastoral internship is not something that is done merely to fulfil a requirement, but will really allow those in charge of the seminarian's formation and the seminarian himself to know his strengths and areas of needed growth in ministry and demonstrate whether a particular seminarian may not be suited for priestly ministry. This assessment provides essential information for the seminarians and for the Church.

Webb (1999) argued for the importance of seminarians' having the full experience of priestly life so that they experience the joys and sorrows of priesthood while being prepared for the real challenges they will face in priesthood should they be ordained (p. 42). Assuring that seminarians are prepared for ministry is important for the good of the People of God: "Significant experience with the people who will be parishioners is essential before ordination" (Webb, 1999, p. 42).

Davies (1999) describes the pastoral internship at St. Augustine's Seminary in Toronto in some detail. He comments that his seminary's pastoral year (a "supervised pastoral internship," taking place after the second of four years of theological study) "is always a watershed in [seminarians'] growth" (p. 47). Among the areas of growth that Davies (1999) indicates as typical during the internship year are seminarians knowing what they are and are not capable of doing, appreciating the ups and downs of rectory life, connecting the spiritual and pastoral aspects of priestly ministry, recognizing the need for taking care of themselves physically, being aware of the need for "responsible celebration as part of the clerical life … engaging freely yet prudently in the food and alcohol provided," internalizing the commitment to pray the Liturgy of the Hours, developing a sense of responsibility, overcoming procrastination, and accepting the call to diocesan priesthood (as opposed to religious life) (p. 52). All these areas link up well with the hope expressed by the other authors considered in this section, that seminaries will find a way to help seminarians taste priestly life, to help them and the seminary discern their call more deeply and to provide them with tools to succeed in ministry.

Another study of seminary formation called for more practical pastoral formation in the Catholic seminary experience because of the evidence of limited preparation of seminarians and young priests for pastoral leadership and administration (Clements, 2000, pp. 26–31). While this study supports the need for the pastoral internship, it is an experience that needs to be integrated into the whole of seminary formation; few seminaries provided serious preparation for the skills that priests need in order to be ready to lead parishes, outside of the pastoral-year internship and one or two classes in this area (Clements, 2000, p. 30). Clements (2000) noted no indication, at that time, that pastoral-year experiences were followed up by significant opportunities to develop seminarians' own parish leadership skills, and he recommended a "'no-holds-barred' evaluation and debriefing following a seminarian's pastoral internship" to help the seminarian grow from the internship into a better spiritual and pastoral leader (pp. 30–31). While Clements' observations about the need for more training in administrative and leadership skills may go beyond the scope of the present study, it is very important to recognize the pastoral internship as a locus where there is some exposure to these essential aspects of priestly ministry.[3]

The evaluation process had previously been considered by Bradesca (1997), discussing methods of evaluation in the late 1990s: "The Pastoral Internship has proven itself to be an interactive learning experience in which local Church membership, the seminary, and the student are mutually engaged in the preparation of the intern, and has contributed to vocational discernment" (p. 61). At the same time, experience without evaluation is not enough; evaluation is an essential part of a good pastoral internship program (Bradesca, 1997, p. 61).

Citing the language used by her own institution, St. Mary Seminary in Cleveland, Ohio, Bradesca (1997) expresses the purposes of such internships, the most typical of which is now the pastoral year:

> Through this learning focused on the exercise of parish ministry, an intern will be better able to discern both his gifts and his growth needs. He

---

[3] As noted above, St. Vincent de Paul Regional Seminary in Florida and St. John's Seminary in California both indicate that parish administration is an important element in their pastoral year internships.

> will experience first-hand the needs of the people and the parish, will test his ability to relate to the people and minister to their needs, and will gain some understanding of the spiritual stamina he needs to sustain himself in ministry (p. 62).

The evaluation process itself is, according to Bradesca (1997), an important part of the formation and discernment of the seminarian, as the man in formation and the seminary staff both see the growth in him and the areas where he needs further growth through the eyes of a variety of evaluators (p. 64). The rite of ordination includes a question from the ordaining bishop, usually answered by the vocations director or the rector of the seminary, about the worthiness of the candidate for orders. The pastoral year is a way to allow the one giving witness to be able to do so with conviction: "No program or process accomplishes it all, but when the local Church engages in a man's preparation for priestly ministry, it seems safe to assume that it is better equipped to 'testify that he is worthy'" (Bradesca, 1997, p. 65).

Some of the recommendations and concerns revealed in extensive research of recently ordained priests, according to Schuth (2002), included, as noted already, a need for deeper prayer life in seminary, as well as more opportunities to work with women, more preparation for parish administration, and more openness about issues of sexuality — in particular celibacy and homosexuality (p. 142). With regards to the need for more preparation for parish administration, she found: "It is conceivable that seminarians could spend more time in parishes during studies and be assigned to an internship year with careful supervision. However, bishops, eager to have men ordained more quickly, are not always keen on another year of preparation" (Schuth, 2002, p. 143). While she also makes other suggestions for things that could be done after ordination, these concerns and Schuth's observations about the reticence of bishops to spend more time (and money) on formation are clearly relevant to this discussion.

Almost twenty-five years ago, Schuth (1996) already acknowledged the difficulty of trying to do all the things different constituencies wanted seminaries to do (p. 188). She mentioned the pastoral year, having CPE and field education during summers, and adding courses. She commented on her findings: "Inserting a pastoral year has been helpful for some students, who return to school with renewed interest and understanding of how and what to study in light of ministerial demands. In other cases, the break in the academic program has proved detrimental to serious study" (Schuth, 1996, p. 188). While some consider it an argument against these internships that many students do not return after the pastoral year, defenders of the program argue that the departure of seminarians during the pastoral year is a sign of its success since it is better to leave during or after the pastoral year than after ordination (Schuth, 1996, p. 188). Two decades later, Schuth (2016) reported that only seven of the 38 theological seminaries she studied require the pastoral year (p. 113). She also indicates that eight seminaries have optional pastoral-year programs.

Part of what inspired my doctoral research was the recognition that it is impossible for a seminary to respond at the same time to all the perceived needs of formation and to the desire for seminarians to be ready for ordination as quickly and inexpensively as possible. Choices need to be made (Schuth 1996, p. 188). Precisely as more requirements are being called for (Congregation for the Clergy, 2016, pp. 28–29, 33–35), recognizing whether anecdotal accounts of the value of some programs over others are accurate acquires ever greater importance. Many of us have positive experience of the effectiveness of the pastoral-year internship, but our examining anecdotal experiences can be of great value. If evidence can be given of the effectiveness of programs, there will be less temptation to eliminate them or dispense with them, as it has been noted that when important requirements are made optional, both seminarians and the Church often end up suffering (Webb, 1999, p. 42).

The pastoral-year internship, as has been seen, seeks to provide an opportunity for a seminarian to put his pastoral skills into use as well as to learn more skills, and to experience parish and rectory life. It is meant to allow an opportunity for deepened discernment on the part of the seminarian, as well as to provide evaluative feedback from supervisors and from parishioners. One of the most important questions that can be answered in the pastoral-year internship is the penultimate question asked of the supervisor (usually the pastor) in the final evaluation at my seminary: "Would you like to have the seminarian assigned to you as a priest one day? Why or why not?" (St. Vincent de Paul Regional Seminary, 2017, p.11).

Priestly fraternity groups

Romano Gómez (2006) comments about the importance of building friendships in seminary: "Now, to the extent that a seminarian feels himself loved, by his formators and his companions, he will have better affective resources to confront his ministerial responsibilities, because he will be able to rely on sufficient elements to develop a mature and integrated personality"[4] (p. 867). A formation activity that seeks to help seminarians grow in the ability to give and receive support in their seminary lives, as well as in their future priestly ministry, is the use of support groups such as Jesus Caritas or Emmaus.

[4] "Ahora, en la medida que el seminarista se sienta amado, por sus formadores y sus compañeros, entonces podrá tener mejores recursos afectivos para afrontar las cargas ministeriales, pues contará con los elementos suficientes para desarrollar una personalidad madura e integrada".

"Friendship is not the whole of the moral life, but there can be no moral and spiritual life without it" (Wadell, 1995, p. 19). Recognizing the importance of friendship in moral and spiritual growth supports the hope that such programs will help seminarians in preparation for priesthood, precisely as they help build bonds among men in formation.

Wadell (1995) describes some of the key factors necessary for friendship: "To be capable of friendship, a person must be marked by a spirit of generosity, which is the opposite of egocentrism, selfishness, and narcissism" (p. 23). Friendships of character or virtue friendships (Aristotle's highest category of friendship) help seminarians to put others first, help to give projects and tasks their proper importance, and are essential to be able to grow to become truly virtuous (Wadell, 1995, pp. 26–27). Two decades ago, Wadell (1995, pp. 28–29) was encouraging seminaries to promote among seminarians the "spiritual friendship" described by Aelred of Rievaulx in which "two or more persons come together to pursue a life of seeking God in Christ."

Seminaries that require or encourage the Jesus Caritas Fraternity of Priests or similar support groups seek to help seminarians value these gifts and prepare them to offer them to others, recognizing the importance of maintaining this type of support in priesthood. The key elements of the Jesus Caritas movement, as it has been implemented at Mount St. Mary's Seminary in Emmitsburg, Maryland, are "call to holiness, mutual spiritual assistance, better service to God and His People, meditation on the Scripture and poverty of spirit" (Lavorgna, 2004, p. 1). Many alumni of this seminary who participated in Jesus Caritas as seminarians formed or joined such fraternities as priests, and one seminarian states: "I have found the support and prayers of the group very helpful in my growth as a seminarian, and I would like to continue my involvement once I leave the seminary and begin my priestly ministry" (Lavorgna, 2004, p. 4).

A similar program, based on the spirituality of Jesus Caritas, but not tied directly to the movement, is the Emmaus group format used at St. Vincent de Paul Regional Seminary in Boynton Beach, Florida. Muhr (2013) describes the development process behind the formation of Emmaus groups (p. 48). The predecessor to the current system was called "formation nights," during which groups of seminarians would discuss different topics related to formation in a highly structured way. As Muhr (2013) himself experienced it, "the sessions seemed contrived and artificial" (p. 48). He goes on: "Formation Night seemed like a chore rather than an opportunity to encounter one another and the grace of God in our lives and ministry" (Muhr, 2013, p. 48).

Muhr thus experimented with modelling the session on the review of life practiced in Jesus Caritas priestly fraternities (2013, p. 48). This experiment, attempted first with a group of deacons approaching ordination to the priesthood, was extremely successful from the first attempt. The change from the theoretical to the experiential in the sessions was very positive. Muhr (2013, p. 49) comments on seminarians' experience of these Emmaus Groups (the new name given to these formation nights): "The students participating in these groups are available to God's handiwork because they are prayerfully reflective, vulnerable and trusting."

The Emmaus Group structure involves six to eight seminarians and a faculty moderator, most of whom have been spiritual directors. Though the

Emmaus Group does not occur in the internal forum, these groups maintain a high level of confidentiality. The meetings occur once per month, beginning with a prayer to the Holy Spirit and followed by an opportunity for each group member to share particular graces or challenges of the previous month. The others listen and do not volunteer advice or counsel to the speaker. At the end of each person's sharing, the group spends some time in silent prayer. At the end of the sharing, all are invited to offer a word or phrase that has moved them, from the sharings that have taken place (Muhr, 2013, p. 49). Muhr (2017) describes the rationale for the development of the Emmaus Group format:

> The theological rationale for the groups is grounded in Scripture, especially the story of Jesus and the disciples on the road to Emmaus — how together the two disciples shared their experiences of the passion of Jesus and how Jesus shared with them his interpretation of the scriptures and the meaning of the Resurrection. This conversation on the journey to Emmaus is symbolic for the types of sharing that deepen faith.... I also found a rationale in the *Program for Priestly Formation,* 5th Edition, which

emphasizes over and over again the need for integration, how academics, pastoral experiences, human formation and spiritual formation are meant to be integrated into a person's life, how seminary formation should foundationally affect the way seminarian thinks, what he believes, and how he acts.

Another example of a fraternal support group that invites seminarians to initiate a life of sharing with fellow seminarians and priests in the final stage of seminary formation is the Companions of Christ, an association of diocesan priests and seminarians currently present in the Archdiocese of St. Paul and Minneapolis (Minnesota) and the Archdiocese of Denver. "[T]he Companions are not a religious order. Sharing common life as religious do, as well as developing strong relationships and holding each other accountable, helps alleviate the problem of isolation some diocesan priests face" (Klemond, 2013). The website of the St. Paul and Minneapolis chapter describes the particularities of the life and ministry of the Companions of Christ:

Together with their fellow diocesan clergy,

> members of the Companions of Christ make a promise of obedience to the diocesan bishop and are assigned by him in the typical manner to serve in parishes or other diocesan institutions. The diocesan bishop in turn and as far as possible assigns members of the Companions of Christ to locations which permit them to live as fraternities of at least three members in rectories or other households (St. Paul and Minneapolis Companions of Christ, 2017).

The Companions of Christ describe the purpose of their shared life to be support for each other in "living the priestly vocation with clarity and joy" and to "call each other on toward this priestly holiness which we all seek" (St. Paul and Minneapolis Companions of Christ, 2017). The Denver group describes what is distinct about the group:

> The Companions have events and ways of relating that help to form a particular culture among this group of friends. Celebrating the Lord's Day on Saturday nights, praying and eating together during the week, committing to a common vision

for priestly excellence, vacationing together, and gathering to share our spiritual joys and struggles in a bi-weekly fraternal group are some of the more important ways that we help each other to follow our baptismal call to holiness and our priestly call to service. You could say that our friendship has an express purpose: to help each other to become saints" (Denver Companions of Christ, 2017).

A clear advantage of the Companions of Christ is that seminarians who join already belong to a group after ordination, but a challenge can be the practicality of maintaining the household structure after ordination. A reported benefit of the Emmaus Group format has been a readiness of many of the recently ordained to join priestly fraternity groups after ordination (Muhr, 2013, p. 49), similar to the experience at Mount St. Mary's (Lavorgna, 2004, p. 1). However, other than this anecdotal evidence that priests who took part in such fraternal programs in seminary are likely to join such groups as priests, my review of the research did not find any published documentation the long-term effectiveness of such programs.

Institute for Priestly Formation

Father Joseph Kelly (2015) describes the Institute for Priestly Formation's (IPF) program for diocesan seminarians in this way:

> For 10 weeks diocesan seminarians are given the time and the invitation to deepen their baptismal identity as adopted sons of God and as disciples called to the diocesan priesthood. They do this by entering into a kind of spiritual boot camp, a formation program that is designed to help them to focus on developing a deep and personal relationship to the God who has called them to follow Jesus as a diocesan priest.

IPF's program for seminarians finds its roots in the efforts of two Jesuit priests, one diocesan priest and one consecrated virgin, who in the early 1990s joined to create a program to help in the preparation of diocesan seminarians for priesthood and in continuing formation for diocesan priests (Kelly, 2015). The first summer session took place in 1995 (Kelly, 2015). This program depends heavily on the spirituality of St. Ignatius of Loyola and starts with an eight-day retreat, which has as its purpose "to reclaim their true core identity as adopted sons in baptism, and to respond to the One who has called them into a loving relationship as disciples and future priests" (Kelly, 2015).

IPF's summer experience of spiritual and intellectual formation for diocesan seminarians is based at Creighton University in Omaha, Nebraska (Dwyer & Hogan, 2008, p. 40). On its website, IPF (2016) describes the Summer Program for Diocesan Seminarians as "focusing on the heartfelt experience of God," including the following elements:

> ... growth in holiness through daily prayer, weekly one-on-one spiritual direction and an individually directed silent retreat, interplay between theology and practical faith, integration of sexuality with celibacy as a generative gift from God, discernment for pastoral leadership, summary of growth and blessings, apostolic service, appreciation of the unique identity of diocesan priests, contemplative leisure.

IPF describes its vision as "to be a center of renewal and resource for the Roman Catholic Church inviting all priests to deeper intimacy with God and lives of ministry flowing from God's abiding presence" (IPF, 2014, p. 9). Of these specific areas of focus, several of them causally relate to the hope that seminarians persevere in ministry if they are ordained: an integrated sexuality, discernment, and the specific characteristics of diocesan priesthood (IPF, 2016). Following the six seminarians who participated in the inaugural IPF session, over 2,250 seminarians have taken part from over 70% of Catholic Dioceses in the US (IPF, 2014, pp. 16, 18).

In 1990, a diocesan priest, a Jesuit, and a consecrated laywoman (Father Richard Gabuzda, Father John Horn, SJ, and Kathy Kanavy) met for a retreat at Creighton University in Omaha, Nebraska. After a series of meetings and discussions, they felt a "call within a call … to serve diocesan priests and seminarians in cultivating the interior life of Trinitarian intimacy through teaching Ignatian Spirituality.… [They] imagined a miniature novitiate for diocesan seminarians set apart from regular seminary life" (Horn, 2017, p. 2).

One of the factors that inspired the three founders of IPF was their perception that seminaries in the early 1990s were healthy in terms of the external aspects of teaching, pastoral preparation and community life but lacked an opportunity to go deeper into the spiritual life (Horn, 2017, pp. 2–3). The theological rationale for this program can be found in John Paul's II's call in *Pastores Dabo Vobis* for priests to have a deep spiritual life so that they may help people approach God themselves; furthermore, the founders found that receiving God is the most important thing any person can do (Horn, 2017, pp. 3–4).

A key element in the vision of IPF is that of the identity of the Christian in general and the priest in particular as a child of God. What Williamson (2015) suggests is unique to priestly spirituality in that priests have a mission to enable other Christians to recognize and fulfill their own call as sons and daughters of God (p. 25). While all Christians share in this mission by baptism, priests need to be marked by "a deep experiential understanding of their identity as God's sons that will enable them to lead the faithful into the same knowledge and experience"

(Williamson, 2015, p. 25). Seminarians need to prepare themselves for that role as knowing one's identity in Christ and living out that filial identity with the Father is a lifelong task (Williamson, 2015, pp. 26–28).

IPF conducted a study of the impact of its program on participants, specifically asking "whether seminary spiritual formation such as this can produce measurable changes in thinking and behavior" (Dwyer & Hogan, 2008, p. 37). The program is specific and clear about its objectives, which include growth in holiness, solid devotion to Jesus and Mary, healthy celibate sexuality, a desire for continued studies grounded in the Scriptures, a deeper sense of what it means to be diocesan priests, and a sense of brotherhood among upcoming cohorts of priests (Dwyer & Hogan, 2008, p. 37). A key purpose is "to awaken heartfelt discernment for future priestly ministry as a spiritual physician and spiritual father" (Dwyer & Hogan, 2008:37). The study showed significant growth in almost all areas measured, as indicated by the seminarian participants' evaluation of their spiritual situation and abilities before and after the summer experience

(Dwyer & Hogan, 2008, pp. 39–41).

IPF has borne other fruits. Many priests and seminary formation staff members from the US and other English-speaking countries have taken part in its programs. IPF has also published many books. The Catholic Psychological Association and the Seminary Formation Council are two organizations that have their roots in IPF. My own doctoral research was first one that I found that sought to ask whether IPF has an impact on perseverance in ministry after ordination (Horn, 2017, pp. 5–6). If I might offer a bit of a spoiler alert of material to be offered in a subsequent article, IPF's positive impact certainly appears to be long-lasting.

Language Immersion Programs

Many seminaries in the United States require seminarians to learn a pastoral language (i.e., a language that will help them in pastoral ministry to a particular language group). Spanish is the most common because of the size of the Hispanic population in the American Catholic Church (Ospino *et al.*, 2014:21). Learning a new language can include immersion experiences, which can help seminarians improve their language skills as well as better understand other cultures. One seminary that expects those seminarians whose native language is not Spanish to take part in a six-week immersion program in La Antigua Guatemala, Guatemala, describes the main reason for this activity: "to assist the seminarian in acquiring a pastoral facility in the Spanish language and practical pastoral experience with Hispanic Catholics" (St. Vincent de Paul Regional Seminary Pastoral Language Department, 2017:1). The rationale presents an integrated image of language study, a shared life with host families, opportunities for pastoral ministry, and spiritual activities. The mission statement concludes: "By participating in Mass with the Guatemalan people as well as sharing in local activities and participating in pastoral ministries, the seminarian will gain invaluable experience to help in his future parish ministries with Hispanic Catholics in Florida and beyond" (St. Vincent de Paul Regional Seminary Pastoral Language Department, 2017:1).

In the United States, the study of languages necessary for pastoral ministry, especially Spanish, has been recommended as part of the education of seminarians for many years, in each stage of formation (USCCB, 2006:62, 65, 67, 69, 75). Another example is St. John's Seminary in Camarillo, California, which requires an intensive language immersion program, depending on the particular needs of the student. Among the advantages of this program, according to Clarke (2011b:34) is that "not only do the students have the opportunity to learn a new language and experience a different culture first hand, but they are placed into a situation where they have a chance to face their anxieties and feelings of powerlessness while serving a new and unfamiliar setting." The hope is that these experiences help seminarians to deepen their sense of the universality of the Church while becoming more open to immigrants. Another seminary's immersion experience in the Dominican Republic was found to have changed the seminarians' understanding of cultural differences and their way of looking at the poor (Martinez, 2010:122).

The growth of the Hispanic population in the Roman Catholic Church of the United States has been dramatic in recent decades. Studies conducted in the 1980s found that about 25% of all US Catholics were Hispanic, and about 15% of all parishes in the US served them in some specific way. The most complete study of ministry to Hispanic Catholics in recent years found that approximately 17% of the US population and 40% of Catholics in the United States are Hispanic. This same study reports that about 25% of parishes are working deliberately to serve Hispanics (Ospino *et al.*, 2014:5, 7). The US Catholic Church has a great need for Spanish-speaking priests; 66% of the pastors in Hispanic communities are non-Hispanic whites (Ospino *et al.*, 2014:21). These pastors have received a variety of preparation, but only 13% indicate that they received dedicated formation in seminary to prepare them for Hispanic ministry (Ospino *et al.*, 2014:21).

Davis and Menocal (2005:30–31) argue that a precondition for ordination to the priesthood in the United States should be openness to Hispanics: "Although in a particularly diverse diocese it might be impossible to prepare all priests for every language and culture present, Spanish and Hispanic cultures are so prevalent and so extensive that they must constitute an exception to that rule" (Davis & Menocal,

2005:31). This argument supports the requirement of seminaries that seminarians undergo a Spanish immersion experience, to strengthen their knowledge of Spanish and also to make them more comfortable in Hispanic cultures (Davis & Menocal, 2005:31).

Making reference to the canonical requirements for ordination that speak of the importance of priests being prepared to serve their people, Davis and Menocal (2005:34) insist that it should be an absolute requirement that men ordained to the priesthood in the United States be competent in Spanish because of demographic trends that indicate that a majority of Catholics in the United States will be Hispanic within a few years. They claim that "only such men guarantee the basic right of the faithful to receive from their pastors … the spiritual goods of the Church" (Davis & Menocal, 2005:35). It has been argued in chapter two that perseverance in ministry matters for the good of the People of God; the pastoral language ability of ordained ministers is essential for the same reason.

Figueroa Deck (2010:35–42) writes about the importance of intercultural skills for seminarians and priests, above all to serve the people they are called to serve. After commenting on the growing diversity among seminarians and presbyterates, he observes: "There is an urgent need among priests and seminarians to develop the capacity for effective and appropriate intercultural relations if presbyterates are to be sources of strength, unity and mutual support for bishops and priests" (Figueroa Deck, 2010:37). Reviewing different aspects of growing diversity in the Catholic population of the US, as well as among the priesthood, Figueroa Deck comments that it is important to consider not only the challenges of having to care for those who speak a different language but also to recognize the gift that they are to the Church (Figueroa Deck, 2010:38). While Figueroa Deck's 2010 article focuses more on skills that have to do with understanding and working with different cultural groups rather than specifically targeting acquisition of language abilities, his argument supports the purpose of immersion experiences, which not only teach language skills, but also place seminarians into a different culture and give them an opportunity to grow in respect for those who are different.

Recognizing the many gifts that priests currently

serving Hispanic parishes bring, Ospino *et al.* (2014:30) comment: "Dioceses need to plan carefully to make sure that the next generation of priests and pastors is ready to meet the needs and demands of the Hispanic and culturally diverse communities where they will be serving." It is important that they recognize the need to prepare priests to serve in the languages of other immigrant groups, which may be more prominent in different areas of the country.

In an academic address to her seminary community, Martinez (2015) addressed the importance of communicating well in both English and Spanish for the sake of pastoral mission of the Church in the United States. Martinez (2015) stated: "Besides English, knowledge of Spanish as well as additional languages is definitely considered an asset in serving the people of God. They are our 'pastoral' languages for this reason." Immersion programmes have also been shown to be more helpful than classes for adults seeking to learn a language (Georgetown University Medical Center, 2012).

Besides helping seminarians learn Spanish, immersion experiences can increase their concern for people of that culture. It would be useful to know if priests who have been ordained for some time have a sense that their participation in an immersion experience had such an impact on them. Furthermore, evidence of whether language immersions prepare seminarians to persevere in lifelong priestly service would also help bishops and formation personnel develop appropriate priorities for priestly training.

Theological reflection

The previous sections have offered a brief overview of each formation activity under consideration in this study. In each case, the intention was to provide as accurate a description as possible, as well as offer arguments that have been presented in favor of the use of the program or against it. Theological reflection about the use of these programs will allow for a reasoned evaluation of these formation activities.

In the previous chapter, I suggested that the new relationship of service to the Church established at ordination is an essential thread in a 2,000-year-old tradition supporting the permanence of ordained ministry. The formation activities considered in this chapter aim in different ways to help seminarians prepare for effective ministry as future priests. But do these activities precisely promote a permanent relationship with the People of God? The Congregation for the Clergy (2016) expresses the meaning of this relationship, founded on a relationship with Christ: "The fundamental idea is that Seminaries should form missionary disciples who are 'in love' with the Master, shepherds with 'the smell of the sheep', who live in their midst to bring the mercy of God to them" (p. 4). This relationship with the Church, rooted in the love of Christ, is a permanent nuptial encounter between the priest and the Church — precisely in the way the *Lumen Gentium* describes her: "the People of God, the Body of the Lord and the Temple of the Holy Spirit" (Vatican II, 1964, §17).

CPE, which has been used in seminary formation for the longest time of these five programs, has been subject to many critiques. Does participation in CPE truly help Catholic seminarians know themselves better as ministers? If it does, then it could prepare them to enter a new and permanent relationship with the Church. This is because if CPE helps to develop skills necessary for ministry, it will also serve that relationship. At the same time, the criticisms of CPE bring into question whether it could promote a healthy relationship between the minister and the Church. Furthermore, the fact that seminaries cannot predict and have no control over the kind of supervision at a given CPE site offers additional reason for concern, especially since the *PPF,* 5th Edition, mentions the quality of supervision as paramount (USCCB, 2006, p. 84). McCarron's argument (1981) calling for real theological reflection on the reasons for using CPE in Catholic seminaries still holds true today (pp. 162–163). Indeed, it is important for all involved in seminary formation to carefully consider the purposes and theological rationale of all formation activities. In the present article, if nothing else, I hope to suggest that all seminarians and diocesan officials do theological reflection on the programs we require and promote for seminarians.

If the propaedeutic year truly fulfils the intention of Holy See, to provide "a solid base for the spiritual life and to nurture a greater self-awareness for personal growth" (Congregation for the Clergy, 2016), then it would help seminarians enter into a permanent relationship with Christ and with the Church (p. 28). The adage "One cannot give what one does not have" applies here. As we await more indication from the USCCB about the US Bishops' expectations for the propaedeutic year, the discussion about the two places where a program has been implemented in the seminary should be helpful in preparation for the future.

If a principal purpose of pastoral formation is to help to determine whether the seminarian is prepared for ministry and allow him to experience that ministry as much as possible so that this experience can inform the final stages of discernment (Romano Gómez, 2006), then the pastoral-year internship is tailored to support these tasks (pp. 887–888). In view of a theology of the relationship of the priest to the People of God, seen as a spousal relationship, the internship experience resembles an engagement period, where both parties (seminarian and Church) receive appropriate accompaniment (which will include supervision and evaluation) to see if this relationship is meant to be. It is important in practice, however, to recognize how much of the effectiveness of the supervision and evaluation on the part of the pastor and others assisting the pastor in working with the seminarian will affect the effectiveness of a given internship experience.

The priestly-support groups which have been considered — Jesus Caritas, Emmaus, Companions of Christ — all have similar purposes: "call to holiness, mutual spiritual assistance, better service to God and His People, meditation on the Scripture and poverty of spirit" (Lavorgna, 2004, p. 1). An important question to ask about these activities, as well as about propaedeutic programs, is whether these movements' models of fraternal life and sharing meet the needs of priestly life and ministry today. At the same time, if the relationship with the Church prizes friendships with brother priests, programs that help priests form bonds within the presbyterate would seem to strengthen their union with the whole Church.

The IPF program for seminarians, as noted above, seeks to help seminarians deepen their spiritual life, in order to be able to help people approach God themselves — to know God, in order to be able to share God's love with others. Here the relationship with God's people is clearly linked to the future priest's relationship with God.

Language immersion programmes appear to be, of all these formation activities, the ones least connected to preparing the priest for a permanent spousal relationship with the Church. The purpose of these programmes, however, is precisely to help the seminarian better know the community he will be serving as a priest, particularly those who will most need his special care since they do not speak English. Immersion experiences respond to the call to "go into the peripheries," an oft-repeated theme in the current pontificate, as they teach US seminarians a language they will need to serve the marginalized in the United States (Akin, 2013; Congregation for the Clergy, 2016:43). Whether having this knowledge and the concomitant growth in language skills assists the priest in remaining committed to the bond established at ordination was an important question asked in my research.

This brief theological reflection has examined the six formation activities in terms of how they prepare seminarians to persevere in ministry. I have also speculated on the possible benefits and drawbacks of each activity. In the next chapter, I will share some of the results of my empirical study, but already these reflections help us to consider the relative value of these different formation activities for the formation of priests conformed to the Heart of Christ.

Chapter 3

Seminary Formation Activities: What Impact on Perseverance?

Introduction to the research process

Do the formation activities seminarians take part in during their years in seminary have an impact on their perseverance in ministry after ordination? When my doctoral research project began, my goal was to identify correlations between taking part during seminary in each of the six activities treated in the previous chapter and perseverance in ministry. The activities were Clinical Pastoral Education (CPE), spirituality or propaedeutic year, pastoral-year internship, priestly fraternity groups, Institute for Priestly Formation (IPF), and language immersion programs. As will be seen, invitations to participate in the survey were sent to all priests ordained in the United States in 2005 as well as to priests who had apparently left ministry in their first ten years, who had been ordained between 2003 and 2005. An insufficient number of respondents who had left active ministry returned their surveys for me to meaningfully compare them to priests still actively serving, so statistical conclusions were not possible. At the same time, however, the inclusion of Likert scales about the impact of the six activities on the respondents' seminary formation and future ministry allowed this research to obtain helpful and important data. The data will show that some of the six activities are evaluated more positively than others. These highly rated activities had a markedly more positive impact than others on different aspects of ministerial life, aspects that likely connect with perseverance in ministry. At this particular moment in the life of the Church, this research suggests concrete recommendations for seminary formators, bishops and vocation directors, and seminarians themselves.

Development of the mailing list

The first step in determining the population selected to receive the questionnaire for this study was a review of the *Catholic Directory* (P.J. Kenedy & Sons, 2016, pp. 1739–2026), in which diocesan priests of Latin Rite dioceses ordained in 2005 were selected, and their names and assignments noted. Later, the address of their placements as of the date of this listing was located in the section for each diocese (P.J. Kenedy & Sons, 2016:1–1540). While this search already found some of these priests listed as being on leave or otherwise out of ministry, the population of the priests out of ministry for the ordination classes 2003, 2004, and 2005 was determined by comparing the listing of all priests ordained in those years, from the 2006 and 2016 editions of the *Catholic Directory* (P.J. Kenedy & Sons, 2006:1671–1995; 2016:1739–2026). Lastly, the names of the priests who appeared to be out of ministry were sorted and compared with the necrology for each of the intervening years (P.J. Kenedy & Sons, 2007:2041–2047; 2008:2062–2068; 2009:2063–2069; 2010:2057–2064; 2011:2054–2060;

2012:2049–2055; 2013:2039–2045; 2014:2054–2061; 2015:2054–2060).

Through this process, 365 priests were found who appeared to have been ordained for US dioceses in 2005 and to remain in active full-time ministry. An additional eight priests were listed as retired but were considered to be in active ministry for the purposes of this study, as they appear to have persevered to retirement. One hundred and fifty-six priests from the three classes appear to be out of ministry, with a variety of listings, such as leave of absence, absent, unassigned, or — most commonly — not appearing at all. The review of the necrologies revealed that 15 priests from these three ordination cohorts had died in the intervening years.

Development of the questionnaire

In preparing the questions for use in SurveyMonkey, which were to be a combination of Likert scales and a series of open-ended questions in each section, it became clear that, rather than offering the option of a paper copy and an online copy, it would be best to give all participants the link to the SurveyMonkey questionnaire and use only that method of data collection. One reason for this procedural decision was the need to use logic in deciding which sections of the questionnaire to complete. A paper survey would have required much more effort on the part of participants to determine which sections needed to be completed, depending on the formation activities in which they had participated in and on their ministerial status. That amount of effort seemed unreasonable to expect.

Once the basic design of the questionnaire was completed, a few persons were asked to complete a test version to determine how long it would take to complete and to ask for feedback on it. Several priests ordained more recently than the cohort being studied, including one who has left ministry, were asked to complete the survey. Additionally, students in a course on research methodology at Loyola University Chicago took the survey, pretending to have participated in certain programs and to be in or out of active ministry. The responses from these test subjects helped me to pare down the questionnaire and ask the questions in ways that were more manageable for the participants.

Data collection process

In July 2017, the request to participate in the study, including the consent form, was sent by US Mail to the identified individuals, with a self-addressed stamped return envelope. A total of 525 invitations were sent out. From this mailing, 17 individuals responded, submitting consent forms and apparently completing the survey. Several further efforts were made to reach potential respondents by electronic means, but in the end a total of 43 individuals completed the questionnaire. Out of a potential population of 477, and recognizing that it is most likely that a significant number of this population never received the request to participate, the response rate is close to 9%. Van der Ven (1998) suggests that response of rates of 20–25% are sometimes the best that a researcher may be able to achieve, meaning that the present response rate is very low (p. 142). Although the total number of respondents is low and the results of this research will have to be considered as qualitative rather than quantitative, this study has still yielded much helpful information.

Concern about the sample size and number of responses

Even in treating this study as qualitative research, whether the number of responses is sufficient for making generalized conclusions remains an important question. According to the principle of saturation, in qualitative research, it is possible to reach a point at which sufficient data has been obtained because it is unlikely that further questionnaires, interviews, or other forms of obtaining data will lead to different results (Tay, 2014). This source cites several studies that indicate that between ten and twelve interviews are sufficient for data saturation. Review of the responses received seems to indicate that the respondents are similar to other priests ordained in that time period. At the same time, Tay (2014) argues that saturation is not a sufficient criterion for determining that sufficient research has been conducted: "Rather than requiring researchers to make the highly challengeable claim that data has been or will be collected until saturated, evaluators should instead require researchers to be transparent and detail why he/she/they stopped or will stop collecting data including making known the limitations and constraints faced or anticipated."

In this case, while the data came from one group of individuals, they represent a number of seminaries and dioceses, and they responded to both Likert scale and open-ended questions, perhaps achieving triangulation. As will be seen, the data obtained from the open-ended questions and the Likert scale questions point in similar directions, which argues for the reliability of this study. At the same time, rather than claim that data saturation has been reached, my preference is to offer the results of this study on their merits. Although I would have preferred a much higher response rate, to have expanded the sample group or devised new surveys for a different population would have meant conducting a different research study altogether. Without making any claims for saturation, this study makes an honest and transparent effort to obtain the best information possible under the circumstances and to offer insights about the impact of the six activities on perseverance in ministry.

Empirical-theological data analysis

The most immediately striking aspect of the collected data was that only four of the respondents indicated that they are currently out of ministry. That low number, despite the effort to contact a significant number of priests out of ministry, means that there is clearly insufficient data to make any kind of meaningful comparison between the participation in the formation activities being considered among persevering and non-persevering priests. Table 1 indicates the responses to question 100: "What is your current ministerial status?" For reasons that are unclear, nine respondents did not respond to this question or the other questions asking for demographic data, but there is no indication from the responses, especially the narrative comments, that there are any more than four respondents not in active ministry.

Table 1

Status in Ministry	Number	Percentage
Active ministry	30	88.24%
Resigned from ministry	2	5.88%
On leave	1	2.94%
Left to get married, considers self-suspended rather than having resigned	1	2.94%

The study asked for some demographic data, while promising that the respondents themselves, their seminaries, and their dioceses would not be identified. Twenty-seven of the respondents who indicated year of ordination were ordained in 2005, with two of the others being ordained in 2003 and four in 2004. Although the intention in the study design was that only priests who appeared to be out of ministry from the classes of 2003 and 2004 would be sent a request to participate, some in fact were in ministry when it seemed they were not, and others may have been ordained in a different year than the source document indicated.

The respondents represent 21 seminaries and 30 dioceses. The mean age at ordination of this group was 35, while the median age was 34. Their ethnic distribution is shown in Table 2.

Table 2

Ethnic group	Number	Percentage
Caucasian/European American/White	28	82.35%
Hispanic/Latino	4	11.76%
Asian/Pacific Islander/Hawaiian	1	2.94%
African/African American/Black	1	2.94%

For purposes of comparison, the survey of priests ordained in 2005 (Hoge, 2005) reported that 67% of diocesan priests ordained that year were European American, 10% Hispanic, 12% Asian or Pacific Islander, 4% African or African American (p. 2).[5]

[5] This same source indicates that the percentages in the column from which these are taken should add up to 100%, while these add to 91%. There is no explanation in the text or the data for this divergence.

The same study found that the mean age of diocesan priests ordained in 2005 was 36.9, just two years higher than the mean for this sample (Hoge, 2005, p. 2). The intervening death of a handful of the priests ordained in 2005 could account for part of the difference in the mean age. Thus, the group in this sample seems like the population of those ordained in 2005, if a little younger at ordination and a little less diverse in terms of ethnic background.

Of the 43 respondents, a total of 30 reported taking part in at least one of the six activities treated in this study. Table 3 indicates the programs in which they participated.

Table 3

Activity	Participants
Clinical Pastoral Education (CPE)	19
Fraternal Support Group	8
Institute for Priestly Formation (IPF)	10
Language Immersion Program	12
Pastoral Internship	15
Spirituality or Propaedeutic Year	8
Participated in at least one activity	30

The most useful data points are the Likert scale assessments made by the respondents of each of the programs they participated in and their comments about these formation activities for the open-ended questions. Some of the most helpful aspects of the data will be shared in this article.

Overall evaluation of the formation activities

The following tables present the responses to the questions in which the respondents were asked to provide an overall evaluation of the formation activities in which they participated while in seminary. While statistical tests of this data will not be attempted, given the small sample in each group, the scales themselves, together with the analysis of the data which will be done, added to the comments about the programs which will be considered, present valuable information.

Tables 4–9 present the data regarding the overall evaluation of each of the programs. The most positive overall evaluation is for IPF, with a weighted average score of 8.89 and with none of the participants offering an overall evaluation of less than 8.00.

The second-highest weighted average evaluation is for the pastoral-year internship with a weighted average of 8.18, the only other formation activity with an average evaluation above 8.00. It is noteworthy that six of the fifteen participants in a pastoral-year internship gave the highest possible score on this item, and four scored it as neutral, which already points to an interesting dynamic that will appear also in the participants' comments, that the pastoral-year internships and the other experiences, while they share many common elements, were different from diocese to diocese and seminary to seminary. IPF was the one general exception; it alone is uniform for all participants, regardless of diocese or seminary.

The lowest overall evaluation was given to CPE, with a weighted average of 6.26, with the nearest activity having an average score of 7.08, the language immersion experience. A wide variety of responses in both cases is noteworthy.

Table 4

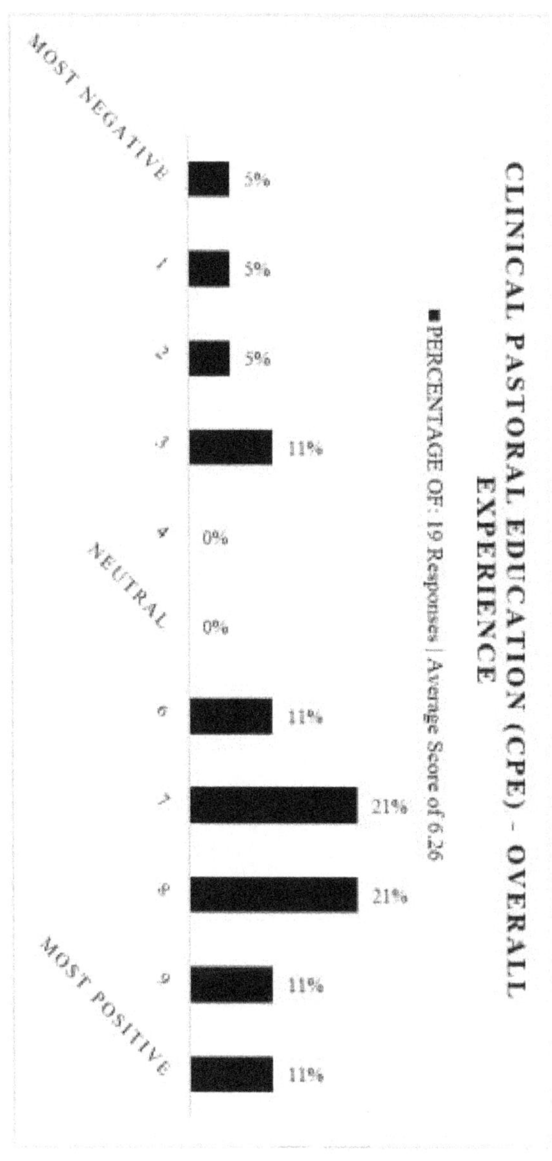
CLINICAL PASTORAL EDUCATION (CPE) - OVERALL EXPERIENCE
■ PERCENTAGE OF: 19 Responses | Average Score of 6.26
MOST NEGATIVE
5%
1
5%
2
5%
3
11%
4
0%
NEUTRAL
0%
6
11%
7
21%
8
21%
9
11%
MOST POSITIVE
11%

Table 5

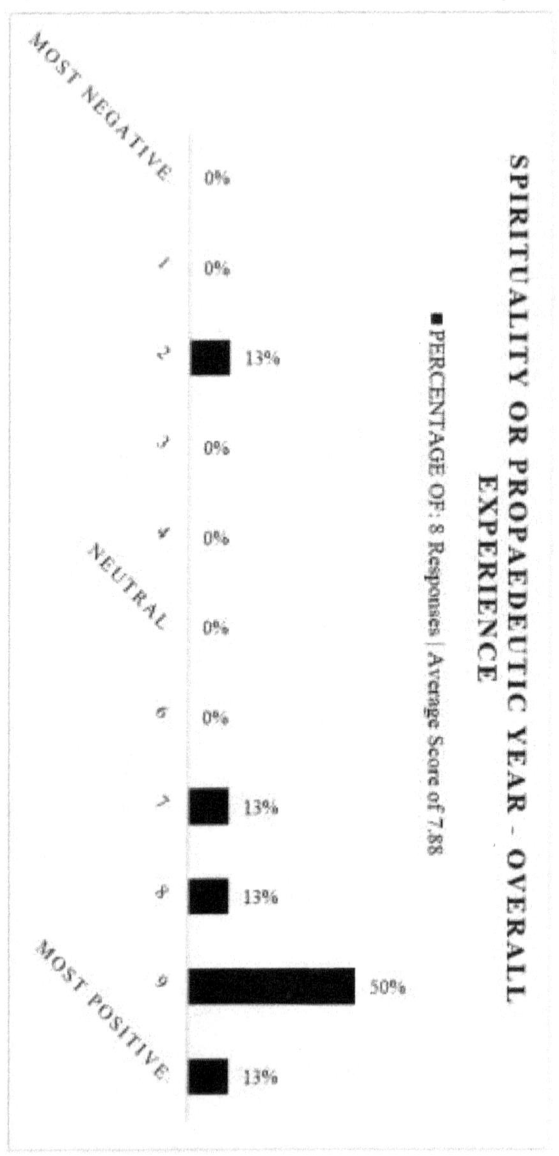
SPIRITUALITY OR PROPAEDEUTIC YEAR - OVERALL EXPERIENCE
■ PERCENTAGE OF: 8 Responses | Average Score of 7.88
MOST NEGATIVE
1
2
3
4
NEUTRAL
6
7
8
9
MOST POSITIVE
0%
0%
13%
0%
0%
0%
0%
13%
13%
50%
13%

Table 6

PASTORAL INTERNSHIP - OVERALL EXPERIENCE
Most Negative
1
2
3
4
Neutral
6
7
8
9
Most Positive
MOST NEGATIVE
0%
1
0%
2
0%
3
0%
4
0%
NEUTRAL
27%
6
0%
7
0%
8
20%
9
13%
MOST POSITIVE
40%

Table 7

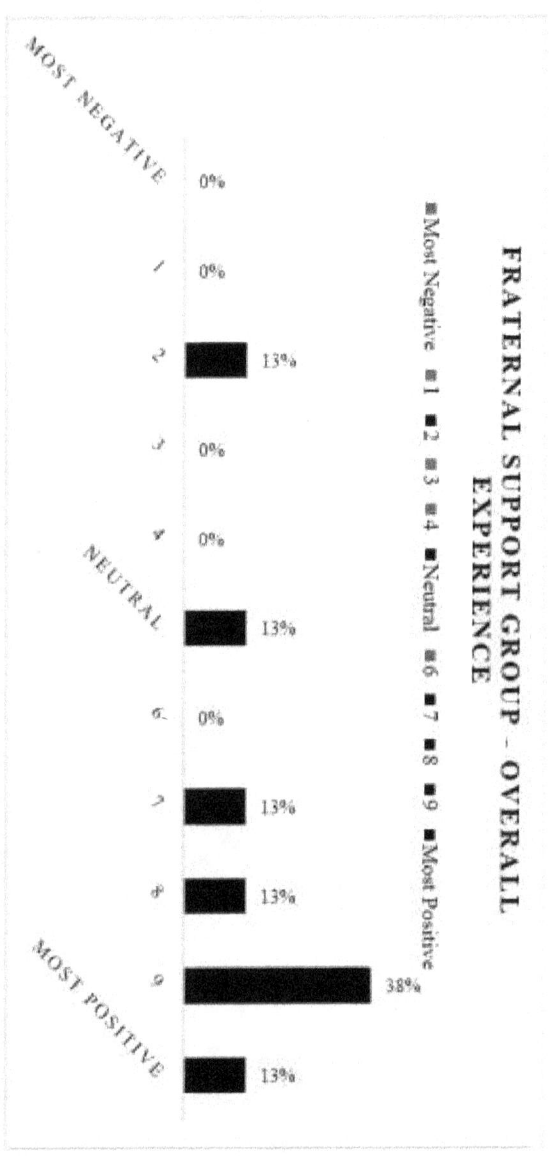
FRATERNAL SUPPORT GROUP - OVERALL EXPERIENCE
Most Negative
1
2
3
4
Neutral
6
7
8
9
Most Positive
MOST NEGATIVE 0%
1 0%
2 13%
3 0%
4 0%
NEUTRAL 13%
6 0%
7 13%
8 13%
9 38%
MOST POSITIVE 13%

Table 8

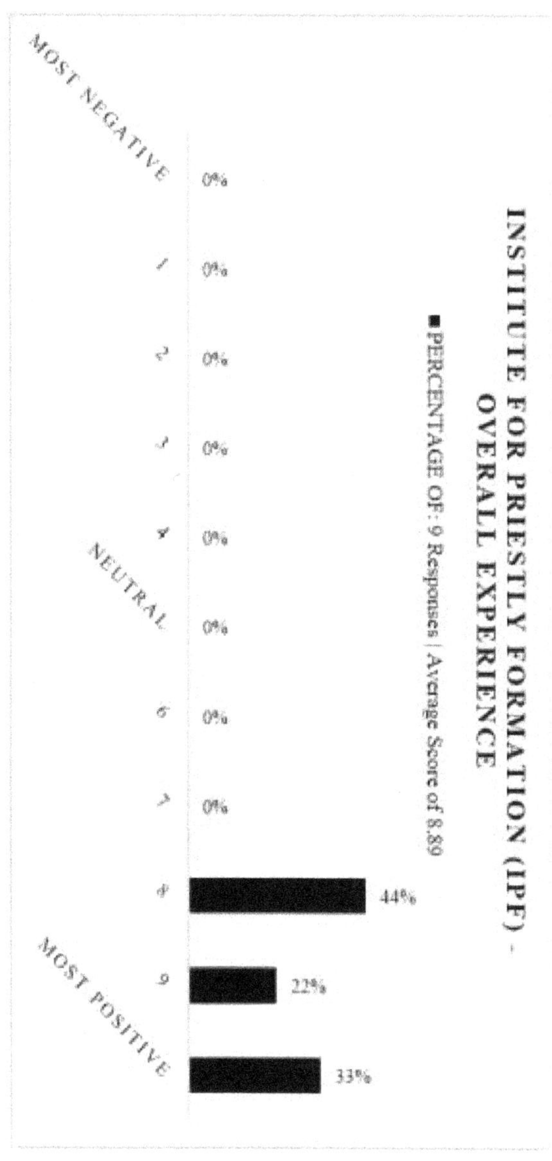
INSTITUTE FOR PRIESTLY FORMATION (IPF) - OVERALL EXPERIENCE
■ PERCENTAGE OF: 9 Responses | Average Score of 8.89
MOST NEGATIVE
1
2
3
4
NEUTRAL
6
7
8
9
MOST POSITIVE
0%
0%
0%
0%
0%
0%
0%
0%
44%
22%
33%

Table 9

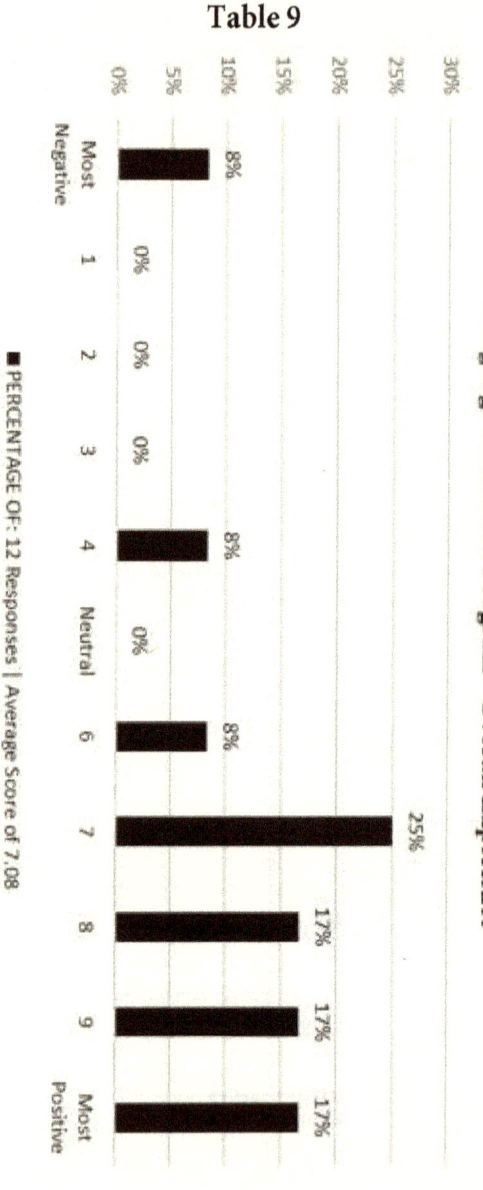
Language Immersion Program - Overall Experience
30%
25%
20%
15%
10%
5%
0%
8%
0%
0%
0%
8%
0%
8%
25%
17%
17%
17%
Most Negative
1
2
3
4
Neutral
6
7
8
9
Most Positive
PERCENTAGE OF: 12 Responses | Average Score of 7.08

Impact of the formation activities on the totality of seminary experience

Similar data could be presented for each of the Likert scale questions. Table 10 presents the average responses to the question about the impact of each formation activity on the totality of the respondent's seminary experience. Once again, IPF scored the highest from the ten respondents who participated in it, with a weighted average of 8.56. Participating in a spirituality or propaedeutic year received the second-highest average score on this question, from the eight respondents who took part in some form of this activity, with a weighted average of 7.88. The fifteen participants in a pastoral-year internship gave this activity the third highest weighted average on this question, 7.73. The presence of some low outliers affected these averages, as on the previous question.

The most negative average evaluation again was for the nineteen participants who took part in CPE, who gave this experience an average score of 5.74 in terms of "the impact CPE had on the totality of their seminary experience." Again, the immersion experience received the second-lowest average score from twelve respondents, of 6.33.

Table 10

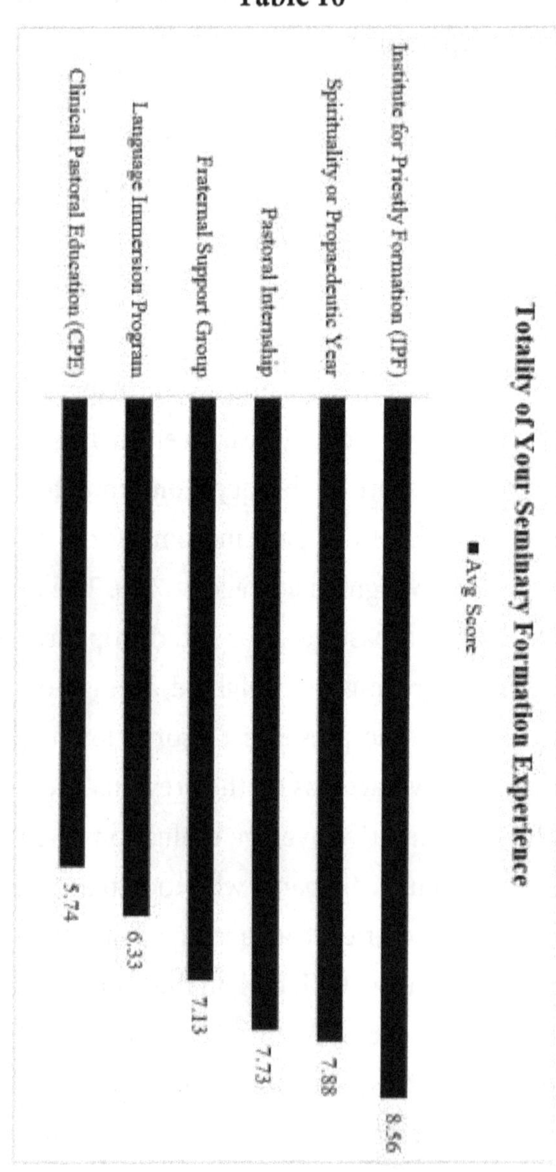
Totality of Your Seminary Formation Experience
Avg Score
Institute for Priestly Formation (IPF)
Spirituality or Propaedeutic Year
Pastoral Internship
Fraternal Support Group
Language Immersion Program
Clinical Pastoral Education (CPE)
8.56
7.88
7.73
7.13
6.33
5.74

Impact of the formation activities on understanding of priestly identity

The respondents' evaluation of the impact of the formation activities on their understanding of priestly identity appears in Table 11. In this case, the highest reported average response was among the respondents taking part in IPF, 9.22, with the second highest average score for the pastoral-year internship, 8.93. Participation in a spirituality or propaedeutic experience ranked third, with an average score of 8.00. CPE, once again, is the lowest ranked formation activity, with an average score of 5.74, with language immersion programs being second lowest, with an average score of 6.25. It is worth noting even before further analysis that language immersion programs would not be expected to have an impact on the understanding of a seminarian's future priestly identity while CPE would be expected to assist in the development of that ministerial identity. In fact, this question was included specifically because CPE's purposes suggested it.

Table 11

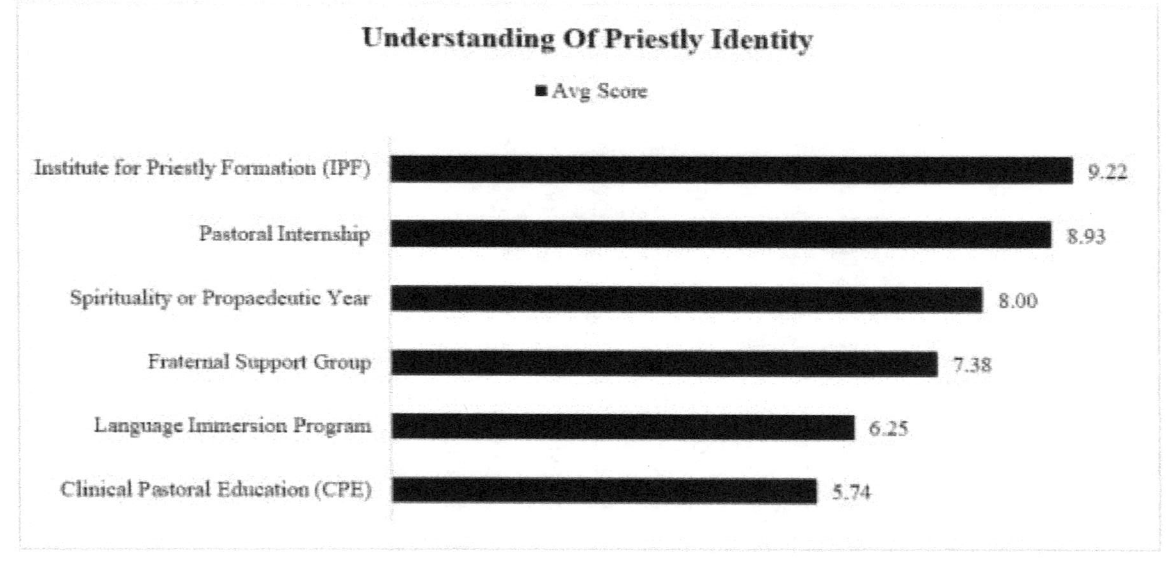
Understanding Of Priestly Identity
Avg Score
Institute for Priestly Formation (IPF)
9.22
Pastoral Internship
8.93
Spirituality or Propaedeutic Year
8.00
Fraternal Support Group
7.38
Language Immersion Program
6.25
Clinical Pastoral Education (CPE)
5.74

The strength of the positive evaluation of IPF and the pastoral-year internship on this variable can be seen in the following tables (Table 12 and Table 13). It is worthy of note that the largest number of respondents rating the program at the highest level is for pastoral year, but the fact that there are some outliers rating the pastoral year less positively makes its mean score lower than IPF.

Table 12

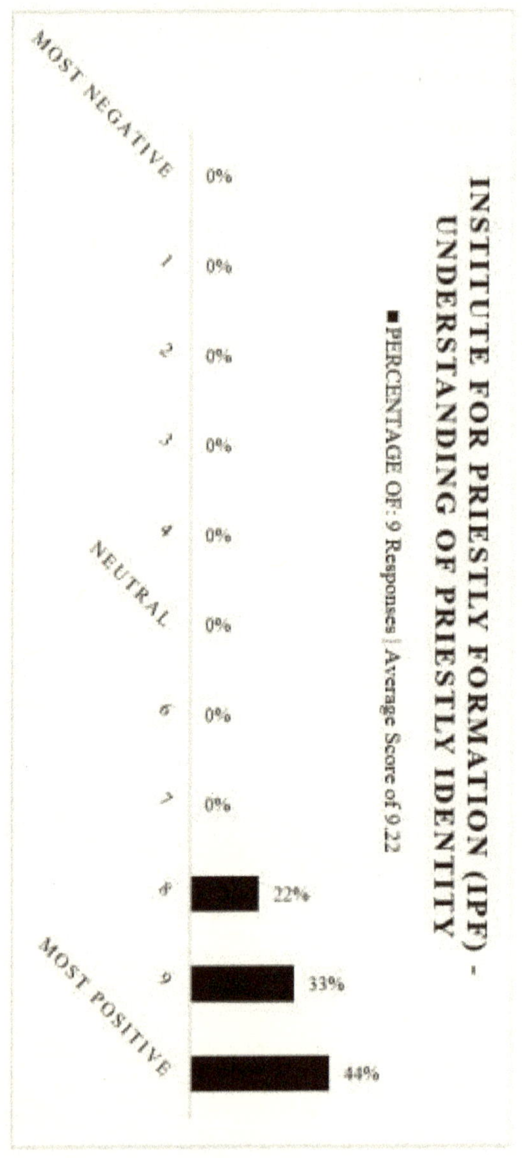
INSTITUTE FOR PRIESTLY FORMATION (IPF) - UNDERSTANDING OF PRIESTLY IDENTITY
■PERCENTAGE OF: 9 Responses | Average Score of 9.22
MOST NEGATIVE
1
2
3
4
NEUTRAL
6
7
8
9
MOST POSITIVE
0%
0%
0%
0%
0%
0%
0%
0%
22%
33%
44%

Table 13

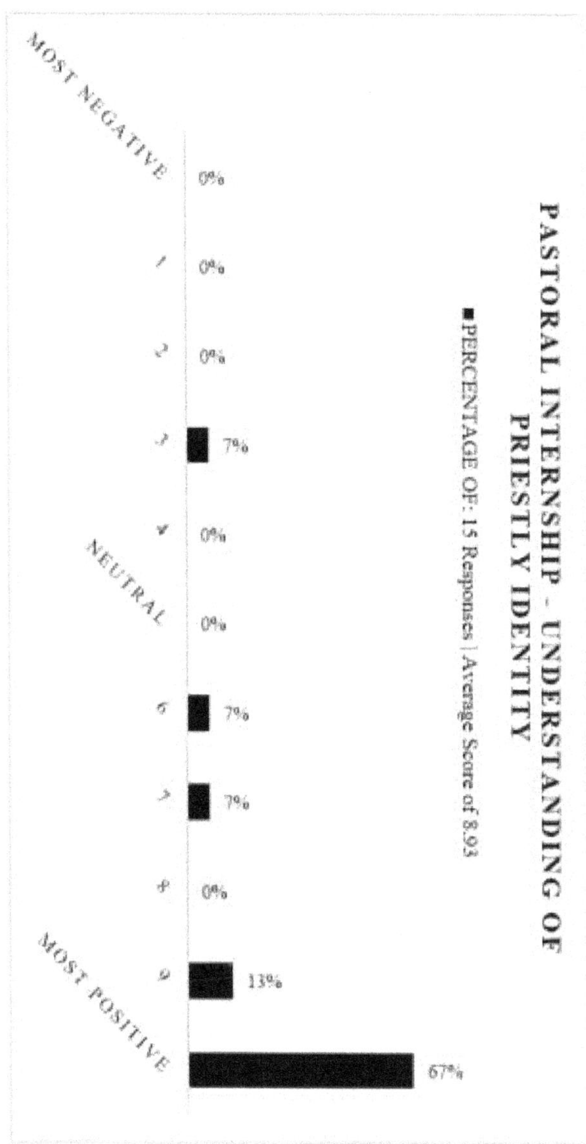
PASTORAL INTERNSHIP - UNDERSTANDING OF PRIESTLY IDENTITY
PERCENTAGE OF: 15 Responses | Average Score of 8.93
MOST NEGATIVE
0%
1
0%
2
0%
3
7%
4
0%
NEUTRAL
0%
6
7%
7
7%
8
0%
9
13%
MOST POSITIVE
67%

The negative evaluation of CPE on this metric can be seen more clearly in Table 14, which presents the individual scores respondents gave to CPE's impact on an understanding of priestly identity. Most of the respondents scored it at neutral or below.

Table 14

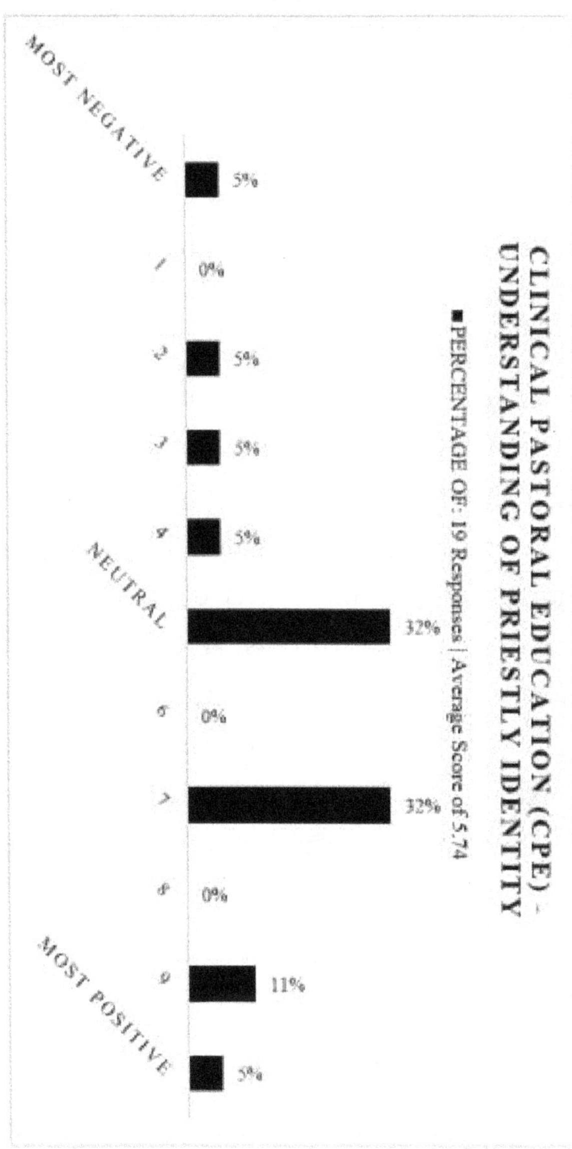
CLINICAL PASTORAL EDUCATION (CPE) - UNDERSTANDING OF PRIESTLY IDENTITY
■PERCENTAGE OF: 19 Responses | Average Score of 5.74
MOST NEGATIVE
1
2
3
4
NEUTRAL
6
7
8
9
MOST POSITIVE
5%
0%
5%
5%
5%
32%
0%
32%
0%
11%
5%

Impact of the formation activities on attitude toward the commitment to celibacy

Before looking at some other ways to look at the data and analyze the findings, it is important to consider one more specific question on the surveys, the question about the effect of the formation activities on the priests' attitude towards their commitment to celibacy. A comparison of the responses to the final Likert scale question appears in Table 15. The commitment to celibacy is of great importance in the Roman Catholic priesthood, and this question sought to measure the impact of these formation activities on the participants' attitude toward this commitment. IPF received the highest average score on this scale once more, 8.50. The second-highest ranking activities are the pastoral-year internship, with a 7.93, and the spirituality or propaedeutic year, with a 7.88. The lowest scores on this scale were a weighted average of 5.16 for CPE and 5.83 for language immersion programs.

Table 15

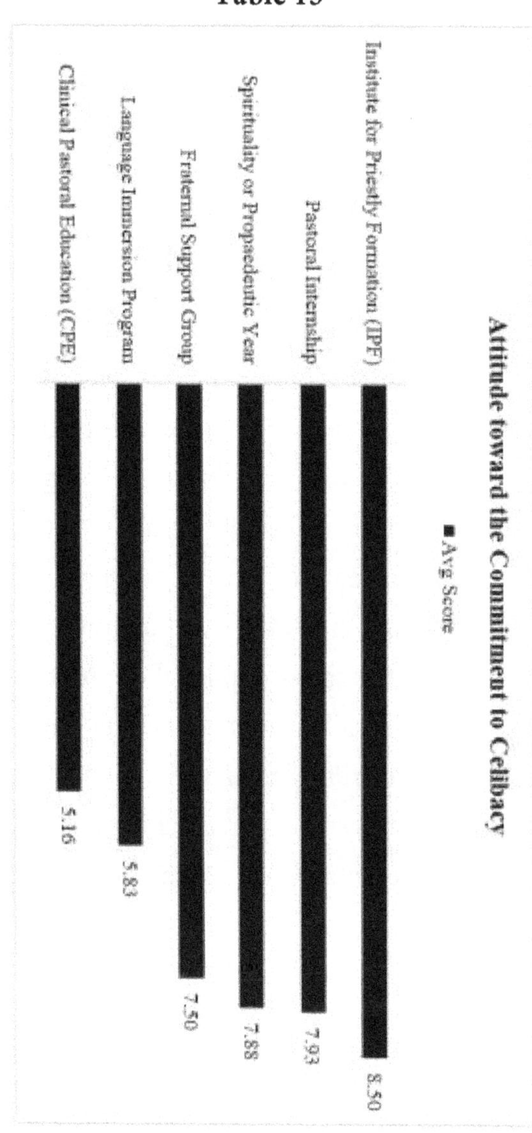
Attitude toward the Commitment to Celibacy
Avg Score
Institute for Priestly Formation (IPF)
8.50
Pastoral Internship
7.93
Spirituality or Propedeutic Year
7.88
Fraternal Support Group
7.50
Language Immersion Program
5.83
Clinical Pastoral Education (CPE)
5.16

Another way to visualize results: Net Impact Score[6]

An approach that has been used in recent years, especially in marketing research, offers a useful way to visualize the results described in this chapter. The Net Promoter Score is a means of analyzing the results of a very specific question: "What is the likelihood that you would recommend Company X to a friend or colleague?" (Bain & Company, 2017). The purpose of this system, which looks at the difference between the percentage of those who give this question an answer of 9 or 10 on a 0–10 scale and those who give a score of 6 or below, is to measure the likelihood of a customer encouraging others to use the service. The top group is called "promoters," the lower group is called "detractors," and those who score at 7 or 8 are called "passives." The "Net Promoter Score is simply the percentage of promoters minus the percentage of detractors" (Bain & Company 2017).

---

[6] I need to give credit to my nephew, Kevin Hernandez, an executive with CableOne in Phoenix, who helped me to interpret the data and who suggested the Net Impact Score as an analytical tool.

While the Net Promoter Score was designed for a business purpose, it is currently used in Catholic research, specifically in the Disciple Maker Index, a survey of parish effectiveness used by the Catholic Leadership Institute (Zlock, 2017; CLI, 2017). In this use of the system, parishes are rated according to a variety of themes, such as spirituality, financial transparency, and faith formation. Comparison with results from other parishes helps parishes to determine areas for improvement (Zlock, 2017).

In the present case, given that the scales being used in the present study are essentially evaluations of satisfaction with how different formation activities affected different aspects of priestly ministry, I used the Net Promoter Score method for each of the questions. Since what is being examined here is not the likelihood of the participants in these formation activities recommending the programs, but the relative impact of each activity on each area of formation, the scale was renamed the Net Impact Score for the purposes of this study. This score represents the difference between the percentage who ranked the specific program with a 9 or 10 on the impact area and the percentage who ranked the program with a score between 0 and 6. This attempt presents the data about the programs in a more dramatic way than in the simple comparisons.

In the following tables, the data from this analysis can be seen. Table 16 offers a key for the following chart, which presents the Net Impact Score for each program and each impact category. This data is presented in Table 17. On this table, the darker shading in green indicates a higher positive Net Impact Score, and the darker shading in red indicates a higher negative Net Impact Score. Table 18 offers a summary, indicating the highest and lowest Net Impact Score for each impact category.

Table 16

Category ID	Impact Category
1	overall experience
2	totality of your seminary formation experience
3	understanding of priestly identity
4	development of a solid base for your spiritual life

5	self-awareness for personal growth
6	development of pastoral skills
7	discernment of call to priesthood
8	attitude towards and participation in support groups
9	attitude towards the spiritual life and maturity in the faith
10	attitude towards and ability to serve diverse communities
11	attitude towards the commitment to celibacy

Table 17

Category ID	CPE	Support	IPF	Language	Internship	Prop.	Total
1	-5	25	56	17	27	50	23
2	-26	0	56	-25	20	38	04
3	-37	25	78	-33	73	50	18
4	-53	0	67	-33	7	50	-4
5	-11	13	44	0	33	0	11
6	-5	0	22	17	53	25	18
7	-68	-13	44	-33	60	50	-1
8	-79	63	33	-50	-7	-13	-21
9	-42	13	44	-25	40	38	4
10	-16	-25	-22	33	7	0	-3
11	-68	25	50	-42	27	25	-7
Total	-37	11	43	-16	31	28	4

Table 18

Category ID	Most Favorable	Net Impact	Least Favorable	Net Impact
1	IPF	56	CPE	-5
2	IPF	56	CPE	-26
3	IPF	78	CPE	-37
4	IPF	67	CPE	-53
5	IPF	44	CPE	-11
6	Internship	53	CPE	-5
7	Internship	60	CPE	-68
8	Support	63	CPE	-79
9	IPF	44	CPE	-42
10	Language	33	Support group	-25
11	IPF	50	CPE	-68

Table 17 helps to point out the activities with the highest positive and negative effects on each aspect of formation. The blocks show either positive Net Impact Scores (the higher the positive number, the more positive the score) or negative Net Impact Scores (the higher the negative number, the more negative the score). IPF has the highest total Net Impact Score, 43, while the pastoral-year intern-ship experience and a propaedeutic or spirituality year experience are in second and third place, with total Net Impact Score of 31 and 28, respectively. The only programs with a negative Net Impact Score are CPE and language immersion programs, with CPE having a much higher negative net impact, –37.

Table 18 presents the most favorable and most negative Net Impact Score for each area of impact. The negative scores are the most dramatic, as CPE ranks lowest in every area, except the ability to serve diverse communities, where fraternal support groups are ranked lowest. As already noted, but shown here in a graph, IPF had the highest net impact in most areas. It is noteworthy that the areas where IPF is not ranked highest, the highest ranking program is specifically related to the area of impact: the pastoral-year internship for development of pastoral skills and discernment of call to priesthood, fraternal support groups for attitude towards and participation in support groups, and language immersion programs for attitude towards and ability to serve diverse communities.

An additional piece of data that this method points out is which areas of impact show a negative total Net Impact Score, when all the programs are looked at together. Even though few candidates would take part in all the programs, the impact areas with negative total Net Impact Score are key areas:

attitude towards and participation in support groups (–21), attitude towards the commitment to celibacy (–7), development of a solid base for the spiritual life (–4), attitude towards and ability to serve diverse communities (–3), and discernment of call (–1). Given how important these areas are for perseverance in ministry, these results indicate the importance of looking at the activities with negative Net Impact Score for these areas of impact, especially those where a positive correlation would be expected.

Narrative responses

The respondents' answers to the open-ended questions about each program also provided helpful information. Given the scope of this article, I will only present a few comments about four of the programs where the discussion to this point of the article has focused, CPE, spirituality or propaedeutic year, pastoral-year internship, and IPF.

CPE

One of the twenty respondents who took part in CPE responded very negatively in describing the CPE experience: "The environment was hostile to sacramental and liturgical theological framework. It was entirely materialistic and psychology-based. The Catholic chaplain at the hospital was off-putting, self-righteous, haughty, and offered no support for the seminarians." Another very negative response, from another priest who is still in ministry, indicated, "CPE was the single worst part of my seven years in seminary. My supervisor was a deeply racist, anti-Catholic woman with severe emotional problems which she inflicted upon me, in particular. If anything, I came out of the program less mature than when I went into it. In short, I hated CPE and everything associated with it."

More positive statements came from several respondents, such as one who indicated: "CPE was invaluable in developing a pastoral identity, forming a ministry of presence, and overcoming fears of difficult situations."

One comment that offers some insight into the

diversity of responses can be seen in a brief response: "I had a great supervisor. I think it makes all the difference." Clearly, CPE experiences vary greatly, depending on location and staff. In describing their programs, the respondents describe very different situations, with regard to the make-up of cohorts, the attitude of supervisors and cohort members toward Catholic theology and pastoral practice, and the qualification of supervisors. This very variety is an important element in discussing the diversity in responses about the efficacy of CPE programs. Seminaries and dioceses have little if any control over the CPE programs they use, which means that relying on this program for the formation of seminarians would be a risky exercise.

Spirituality or Propaedeutic Year

The most important finding relating to the responses to the open-ended questions regarding this kind of program, both describing the activity in which the respondent participated and offering additional commentary, reveals that the eight persons who said they took part in a spirituality or propaedeutic year participated in very different kinds of programs. The question asked: "During your seminary formation, did you participate in a spirituality year or propaedeutic year (an entire year dedicated to spirituality and preparation for full immersion into seminary life)?" Despite the question seeming clear, one participant described a religious novitiate as his spirituality year, another a year in parish, another a summer experience, and another a mentorship with an older priest. Knowing this is important in assessing the comments about the experience and the evaluation made by participants. This diversity of experiences makes it more difficult to assess the impact of these programs on the formation of the respondents.

Pastoral-year internship

The fourteen respondents who took part in a pastoral-year internship described these as ranging from seven to thirteen months. They describe their activities as covering the gamut of parish life, including parish committee, preaching, visitation of the sick, catechesis, working with staff and rectory living.

Different seminaries had different ways of relating to seminarians on internship, from having little contact to having staff make visits to the placement sites and having the seminarians visit the seminary for workshops.

The only two respondents who give a negative assessment of their pastoral internship experiences in their written comments have both left active ministry. One writes: "It just didn't have any community life at all. The rich liturgical life of the seminary was exchanged for truly mediocre parish liturgies. No community with the Pastor or the Associate. Long drive to my family's home. Again, felt as a hurdle to overcome — I felt very under-supported and under-utilized." Another comments that there was not much opportunity to develop skills during the internship and adds the following: "Many of my classmates left the seminary after their pastoral year. In hindsight, I should have as well."

Among the other respondents, several indicate that the pastoral internship was a key moment of formation for them. One indicates that it helped in developing "in self-confidence, the ability to persevere in the priestly lifestyle, and in developing healthy relationships with the laity." Two others say that the internship was important in confirming their discernment of the priesthood, with one writing: "It helped me to make my final decision towards the priesthood."

The diversity of responses here points to the challenge for seminaries using pastoral-year internships. It is essential that seminaries remain connected with their seminarians during the year if it is hoped that it will be year of intentional formation. The danger of leaving the formation that occurs to the luck of the draw of pastor and placement is that when these go wrong, they can go very wrong. If the seminary is involved each step of the way, everything that happens is formational.

Institute for Priestly Formation (IPF)

It is noteworthy that all nine respondents who indicated that they participated in IPF are still in active ministry. Of the five who offered responses to the open-ended question, one affirmed the quality of the program, but wrote, "I felt it was geared towards earlier stages in formation." At the same time, another participant found that going through IPF immediately after his pastoral internship "provided an optimal time of discernment for the priesthood." One respondent stated that the thirty-day retreat that IPF offers was of immense importance to him. A high level of appreciation for the program is expressed in this response: "Highly recommend IPF and if I were vocations director would probably require all seminarians to attend."

Conclusion

When I began my research, my initial hope was that my research would provide the answer to the question about the relationship between participation in each of the programs to be studied and perseverance in ministry. While the number of respondents and specifically the number of respondents out of ministry is too low to answer this question directly, the data collected does point to the impact of some of the programs being considered on some key areas of attitudes and skills for success in ministry, in some cases positive and others negative.

Clearly, the most positive overall evaluation is of IPF and pastoral-year internships. It is also evident that the most negative overall evaluation is for CPE. Similar results were obtained for the question about the impact of the various formation activities on the totality of the seminary experience and on the understanding of priestly identity, with IPF being ranked highest, with the difference that the spirituality or propaedeutic year is ranked second highest in the first case with the pastoral internship in third place, and the results being reversed for priestly identity. These questions relate to essential parts of seminary formation, so the positive and negative evaluations of the impact of individual formation activities are important to note.

It is not surprising that the pastoral-year internship is evaluated as most effective for the development of pastoral skills. The very high ranking for the pastoral-year internship, with IPF in second place, is of great importance in considering the importance of these programs, since without the skills for competent ministry, frustration will result. One of the recommendations made by recently ordained priests is for more "practical hands-on training during seminary" (Hoge, 2002, p. 93). No experience is more hands-on than the pastoral internship. It appears ironic that CPE, which focuses very much on skills for hospital ministry, ranks lowest on this scale as on most of the others.

Discernment of a true vocation is clearly an essential aspect of making a permanent commitment. Thus, the ranking of IPF and the pastoral-year internship as the activities receiving the highest average response to the question about the impact on discernment, by both the seminarian and the seminary formation team, is important. CPE's very low rating (4.84), as has been noted, stands out since CPE would be expected to help participants to know themselves better, a key aspect of discernment.

The one impact question where fraternal support groups ranked highest is attitude towards seeking the support of other priests in such groups after ordination. It is similarly noteworthy that the language immersion programs are ranked highest for the attitude towards and ability to serve diverse communities. In both areas, the activity most associated with these hoped-for results indeed appears to be effective in producing them. It is important to look at the other results for these programs, in making suggestions as to how to best use them, so that they will be effective and integrated parts of the formation process.

The last of the questions to consider, the attitude towards the spiritual life and maturity in the faith is again one in which IPF received the highest evaluation, with the spirituality or propaedeutic year and the pastoral internship ranking second and third, respectively. Fraternal support groups also received a strong evaluation here. Once again, CPE was ranked lowest. It is interesting to note, given the connection between the spiritual life and the capacity for chaste celibacy, that the scores for the final impact area, commitment to celibacy, are similar. The recommendations Hoge (2002) presents from priests both in and out of ministry begin specifically with the need to be more open about sexuality, including celibacy and sexual orientation, in seminary formation (pp. 96–98). If these programs help to accomplish this in a positive and effective way, then they are certainly helpful.

To summarize, the very positive impact of IPF and the relatively positive impact of pastoral internship and spirituality or propaedeutic year programs stand out, in looking at all the data discussed in this chapter. A striking detail is that IPF is one program in one location, easily able to maintain quality control. While some ranked their experience of the pastoral internship or a spirituality year very high, these programs differ highly in each location, which makes comparison difficult across different experiences, even if the basic purposes are similar. If this holds true for the activities with positive overall impact scores, the data for other activities have the same limitation: not only are there different perceptions from participants in the same program, but the elements and quality of the program may vary significantly from place to place.

An analogy may help to illustrate the differences. There may be a particularly good restaurant that consistently gets rave reviews so that people come from all over to eat there. There may be another good restaurant that gets rave reviews and opens franchises in different towns. Even though they plan on serving the same menu, the franchisees have a great deal of freedom, which means the quality is significantly different from one location to another. Some may be better than the original, while others may be worse. Finally, there is another restaurant that is exceptionally good, and others try to imitate it in other towns, but there is no specific connection to the original restaurant, so that there is very little resemblance sometimes to the original.

What could be called a "franchise effect" may be one factor in the differing degrees of impact measured among these programs. Although no assessment of statistical significance can be made, this data, considered as qualitative data, is certainly suggestive. Another question is whether the basic purpose of an activity fits Catholic formation. The responses offered in this study about CPE, the activity in which twenty respondents participated — the largest number of any of the formation activities — received the most negative comments and the lowest scores, both in the scaled responses and in the open-ended questions. A relevant question is whether CPE should have a place in Catholic seminary formation today, given the data in this article and the information I presented in my previous article. The analogy of the restaurant could be extended to ask whether the food offered at this particular restaurant, regardless of which franchise one goes to, is something that these customers want.

One theological question suggested by the data is what differentiates the formation activities with the more positive evaluations from those with the lowest rankings. It is worthy of note that IPF, the pastoral-year internship, and the spirituality or propaedeutic year experiences all have the formation of priests for successful ministry as their primary purpose. Fraternal support groups, ranked next in order, are run in different ways in different seminaries (cf. the franchise effect noted earlier), but its purpose is also clear. Language immersion programs and CPE are used by seminaries and dioceses for their seminarians for narrower purposes, but they, as a whole, do not have the formation of Catholic clergy as a significant goal. Intentionality matters. To use an analogy, if the carpenter did not specifically intend to make a chair, it is unlikely a chair will be built.

In my dissertation (Hernández, 2019), I suggested that it would be good for an organization with the resources and the reputation of the Center for Applied Research in the Apostolate (CARA) to undertake this kind of research. Since CARA already conducts research into each graduating class of US seminaries, it could include questions about participation in different formation activities in seminary in the annual survey (p. 191). Longitudinal comparisons after ordination would provide good information about factors that appear to promote perseverance or not. In fact, thanks to discussion among the National Association of Catholic Theological Schools and the USCCB's Committee on Clergy, Consecrated Life and Vocations, the latest edition of the CARA survey of the 2019 ordination class did in fact include questions about these formation activities (Gautier & Do, 2019, p. 44). This addition will make it much easier for a future study of this kind to have good data for a thorough study of the long-term impact of different programs on priestly perseverance and ministerial effectiveness.

The permanence of priestly ministry is not only a matter of dogmatic theology alone. As we saw in chapter one, perseverance matters to the People of God. Seminaries and dioceses in the United States should choose programs for their seminarians that have been shown to assist them in preparing for effective and persevering ministry. The well-being of seminarians and priests, as well as the good of the people they are being prepared to serve, calls for an attentive reading of the results of this study, as well as for additional research. It is my hope that this research will indeed lead to the improvement of the programs seminarians use and to the selection of those programs that will help the most in helping priests to be joyful, faithful, and fruitful in their ministry. In seminary work, we talk a lot about the importance of helping seminarians do theological reflection about their pastoral activities. May all of us involved in seminary formation do serious theological reflection about the programs into which we invest the money of our dioceses and seminaries and the time and the lives of our seminarians.

Bibliography

Association of Theological Schools (ATS). 2016. 2015-2016 annual data tables. http://www.ats.edu/uploads/resources/institutional-data/annual-data-tables/2015-2016-annual-data-tables.pdf. Date of access: 29 May 2016.

Augustine of Hippo. (1994a). On baptism, against the Donatists. (J.R. King, Trans.). In *Nicene and post-Nicene Fathers, first series, vol. 4* (pp. 407–514). Peabody, MA: Hendrickson.

Augustine of Hippo. (1994b). On the good of marriage. (C.L. Cornish, Trans.) In *Nicene and post-Nicene Fathers, first series, volume 3* (pp. 395–413). Peabody, MA: Hendrickson.

Bain & Company. 2017. Net Promoter System©. Retrieved on November 9, 2018 from http://www.netpromotersystem.com/about/why-net-promoter.aspx.

Ballard, P. & Pritchard, J. (1996). Practical theology in action: Christian thinking in the service of church and society. London: SPCK.

Bradesca, D. 1997. Evaluation and the pastoral internship. *Seminary Journal*, 3(1), 61-101.

Camelli, L.J. 2008. Called, formed, sent: how seminaries can foster lifelong learning and ongoing formation. *Seminary Journal*, 14(2), 15-22.

Catholic Leadership Institute. 2017. Supporting special projects. Retrieved on November 30, 2018 from http://www.catholicleaders.org/home.aspx?pagename=SupportingSpecialProjects.

Clarke, J. 2011a. Immersion experiences as a learning tool for seminary formation. *Seminary Journal*, 17(1), 32-34.

Clarke, J. 2011b. Another look at seminary formation. *Seminary Journal*, 17(1), 29-31.

Clement of Rome. (1994). The first epistle of Clement to the Corinthians. In A. Roberts & J. Donaldson (Eds). *Ante-Nicene Fathers, volume 1* (pp. 1–21). Peabody, MA: Hendrickson.

Clements, C.J. 2000. Stools or tables? The missing leg of ministry preparation. *Seminary Journal*, 6(3):26-31.

Congregation for the Clergy. 2016. The gift of the priestly vocation: *ratio fundamentalis institutionis sacerdotalis*. Vatican City: L'Osservatore Romano.

Davies, G.F.1999. "Living with Wisdom" (Wis 7:28): Areas of Growth in Spiritual Formation, Year by Year. *Seminary Journal*, 5(3), 47-56.

Davis, K.G. & Menocal, L. 2005. "Culled" to worship? priestly formation and Hispanic ministry. *Seminary journal*, 11(3), 30-37.

Denver Companions of Christ. 2017. Retrieved April 12, 2017, from http://www.denvercompanionsofchrist.org/.

Dwyer, K.K. & Hogan, E. 2008. Assessment of the summer programme of spiritual formation for diocesan seminarians: pre- and post-self-report measures indicate significant change. *Seminary Journal*, 14(3), 37-41.

Elliott, J.H. (2000). Anchor Bible: 1 Peter: a new translation with introduction and commentary. New York: Doubleday.

Ferraro, G. 2006. L'identità del presbitero: intreccio tra cristologia ed ecclesiologia nel magistero del Papa Giovanni Paolo II. *Seminarium*, 46(4), 749-788.

Figueroa Deck, A. 2010. Intercultural competence and the priestly vocation. *Seminary journal*, 16(3), 35-42.

Froehle, B. 2011. Research on Catholic priests in the United States, since the Council: modeling the dialogue between theology and social science. *U.S. Catholic Historian*, 29(4):19-46.

Gaillardetz, R.C. (2003). Ecclesiological foundations of ministry within an ordered communion. In S.K. Wood (Ed.). *Ordering the baptismal priesthood: theologies of lay and ordained ministries* (pp. 26–51). Collegeville, MN: Liturgical Press.

Garrido, A.M. 2010. A Catholic vision of theological field education: glimpses from the ministry formation documents. *Seminary Journal*, 16(3), 30-34.

Gautier, M.L. and Do, T.T. 2019. The Class of 2019: Survey of ordinands to the priesthood. Washington, DC: Center for Applied Research in the Apostolate.

Geany, D.J. 1965. Social action in seminary education. In Lee, J.M. & Putz, L.J., Eds. *Seminary education in a time of change.* (pp. 479-505). Notre Dame, IN: Fides.

Georgetown University Medical Center. 2012. In immersion foreign language learning, adults attain, retain native speaker brain pattern. https://www.sciencedaily.com/releases/2012/03/120328172212.htm Date of access: 21 Feb. 2017.

Google. 2017. Search results for "Catholic, seminarian, CPE". Retrieved on January 17, 2017, from Google search.

Griffin, C. (2019). Why celibacy? Reclaiming the fatherhood of the priest. Steubenville, OH: Emmaus Road.

Hemenway, J. 2005. Opening up the circle: next steps in process group work in Clinical Pastoral Education (CPE). *The Journal of Pastoral Care & Counseling*, 59 (4), pp. 323-334.

Hernández, A.I. (2019). Formation activities and Catholic seminarians: A Practical theological study of their impact on subsequent perseverance in ministry. Potchefstroom, South Africa: North-West University. (Dissertation — PhD).

Hoge, D.R. (2006). Experiences of priests ordained five to nine years. Washington, DC: National Catholic Educational Association.

Horn, J. 2017. Institute for Priestly Formation [personal communication]. 22 Feb., Boynton Beach, FL.

Hünerman, P. (Ed.). (2012). Heinrich Deniziger: Compendium of creeds, definitions, and declarations on matters of faith and morals, forty-third ed. San Francisco: Ignatius Press. (Citations to page and paragraph number.)

Ignatius of Antioch. (1994). The epistle of Ignatius to the Ephesians. In A. Roberts & J. Donaldson (Eds.) *Ante-Nicene Fathers, volume 1* (pp. 66–72). Peabody, MA: Hendrickson.

Institute for Priestly Formation. 2014. *Vision for the future*. Omaha, NE.

Institute for Priestly Formation. 2016. *Summer program for diocesan seminarians*. Retrieved on August 18, 2016 from http://priestlyformation.org/programmes/summer-programme-for-diocesan-seminarians.html.

Irenaeus of Lyons. (1994). Against heresies. In A. Roberts & J. Donaldson (Eds.) *Ante-Nicene Fathers, volume 1* (pp. 309–567). Peabody, MA: Hendrickson. Hubbard L. & Robbins, M.R. 2017. St. John's Seminary pastoral internship program [personal communication]. 26 Feb., Camarillo, CA.

Lutheran World Federation and Pontifical Council for Promoting Christian Unity. 1999. Joint declaration on justification. http://www.vatican.va/roman_curia/pontifical_councils/chrstuni/documents/rc_pc_chrstuni_doc_31101999_cath-luth-joint-declaration_en.html Date of access: 11 Aug. 2016.

John Chrysostom. (1994). Treatise concerning the Christian priesthood. (W.R.W. Stephens, Trans.). In *Nicene and post-Nicene Fathers, first series, vol. 9* (pp. 25–83). Peabody, MA: Hendrickson.

John Paul II (Pope). 1992. *Pastores dabo vobis.* Retrieved on June 17, 2016, from http://w2.vatican.va/content/john-paul-ii/en/apost_exhortations/documents/hf_jp-ii_exh_25031992_pastores-dabo-vobis.html.

Johnson, L.T. (2001). *The First and Second Letters to Timothy.* New York: Doubleday.

Kelly, J. 2015. Spiritual boot camp: good news from the Heartland for diocesan seminarians. *OSV News weekly.*

Klemond, S. Companions of Christ celebrate 20 years of priestly fraternity. 2013. *National Catholic register.* Retrieved on April 22, 2017, from http://www.ncregister.com/site/article/companion

s-of-christ-celebrate-20-years-of-priestly-fraternity.

Lavorgna, J.L. 2004. Jesus Caritas: experiencing fraternity for the sake of Jesus and his Gospel. *Mount Saint Mary's: A Newsletter for Alumni and Friends*, 8(4), 1,4.

Little, N.K. 2010. Clinical Pastoral Education as professional training: some entrance, curriculum and assessment implications. *Journal of Pastoral Care & Counseling* 59(4), 228-232.

Luther, M. (1523). Concerning the ministry. (C. Bergendoff, Trans.). In Bergendoff, C. (Ed.) 1966. *Luther's works: church and ministry, vol. 2* (pp. 3–44). Philadelphia: Fortress Press.

Martinez, J. 2010. Evaluation of a pastoral language programme at a Roman Catholic theologate seminary. Fort Lauderdale, FL: Nova Southeastern University. (Dissertation – EdD).

Martinez, J. 2015. Academic Convivium address for St. Vincent de Paul Regional Seminary. (Unpublished).

McCarron, G.J. 1981. Roman Catholic Seminaries: The pragmatic motivations behind involvement in the CPE movement and the ecclesiological and educational implications of these motivations. Princeton,

NJ: Princeton Theological Seminary. (Dissertation — PhD).

Mount Angel Seminary. 2015. Rule of life. Retrieved on January 11, 2017 from https://www.mountangelabbey.org/seminary-catalog/.

Muhr, M. 2013. Emmaus Groups in seminary formation: an experience of fraternity and faith sharing. *Seminary Journal*, 19(1), 48-49.

Muhr, M. 2017. Emmaus groups — response to questionnaire [personal communication]. 28 Mar., Tampa, FL.

Osborne, K. (1988). Priesthood: a history of the ordained ministry in the Roman Catholic Church. New York: Paulist Press.

Osmer, R. (2008). Practical theology: an introduction. Grand Rapids, MI: William B. Eerdmans.

Ospino, H. 2014. Hispanic ministry in Catholic parishes a summary report of findings from the *National study of Catholic parishes with Hispanic ministry*. Boston: Boston College School of Theology and Ministry.

P.J. Kenedy & Sons. 2000-2015. The official Catholic directory. Providence, NJ.

Pius XI. (1935). *Ad catholici sacerdotii*. Retrieved July 19, 2016 from http://w2.vatican.va/content/pius-xi/en/encyclicals/documents/hf_p-xi_enc_19351220_ad-catholici-sacerdotii.html.

Powell, P.N. 2009. Seminarians: do not be bullied (updated). *Domini, da mihi hanc acquam* (blog). Retrieved on January 10, 2017 from https://hancaquam.blogspot.com/2009/03/seminarians-do-not-be-bullied.html.

Powell, R. 2005. Guest editorial: "The challenge to our seminaries – worldwide." *Journal of Pastoral Care*, 59 (4), pp. 317-321.

Rafferty, J. 2011. Pastoral formation in light of Jesus' intimate bond with the Father. *Seminary Journal*, 17(2), pp. 32-38.

Ragsdale, J., Holloway, E. & Ivy, S. 2009. Educating CPE supervisors: a grounded theory study. *The Journal of Pastoral Care & Counseling*, 63(3,4), pp. 10, 1-14.

Ravitz, J. 2015. From girlfriends to God: seminarians answer the call. 26 Sep. 2015. Retrieved on May 26, 2016, from http://www.cnn.com/2015/09/22/us/philadelphia-catholic-seminarians/.

Romano Gómez, M. 2006. La dimensión pastoral de la formación sacerdotal. *Seminarium*, 46(4), pp. 847–892.

Rossetti, S.J. 2011. Why priests are happy: a study of the psychological and spiritual health of priests. Notre Dame, IN: Ave Maria.

St. John Vianney Theological Seminary. 2016. *Spiritual Year Formation Booklet.*

St. Paul and Minneapolis Companions of Christ. 2017. Retrieved on April 12, 2017, from http://www.companionsofchrist.org/ Date of access: 12 Apr. 2017.

St. Paul Seminary School of Divinity, Department of Pastoral Formation. 2013. *Spiritual Pastoral Ministry Manual.* (Unpublished.)

St. de Vincent Paul Regional Seminary. 2016. *Catalog.* Boynton Beach, FL: St. Vincent de Paul Regional Seminary.

St. de Vincent Paul Regional Seminary. 2019. *Catalog.* Boynton Beach, FL: St. Vincent de Paul Regional Seminary.

St. Vincent de Paul Regional Seminary. 2017. Pastoral formation rubric for pastoral year. (Unpublished.)

St. Vincent de Paul Regional Seminary Pastoral Language Department. 2017. Spanish language immersion program. (Unpublished.)

Schuth, K. 1996. Reason for the hope: the futures of Roman Catholic theologates. Wilmington, DE: Michael Glazier.

Schuth, K. 2002. The study's implications for seminary formators. In Hoge, D.R., Eds. 2002. *The first five years of priesthood: a study of newly ordained Catholic priests*. Collegeville, MN: Liturgical Press. pp. 139-145.

Schuth, K. 2016. Seminary formation: recent history, current circumstances, new directions. Collegeville, MN: Liturgical Press.

Tay, I. 2014. To what extent should data saturation be used as a quality criterion in qualitative research? Retrieved on November 20, 2017 from https://www.linkedin.com/pulse/20140824092647-82509310-to-what-extent-should-data-saturation-be-used-as-a-quality-criterion-in-qualitative-research.

Thermos, J. 2017. Spirituality year: response to questionnaire [personal communication]. 19 Feb., Denver, CO.

Toups, D. (2004). The sacerdotal character as the foundation of priestly life: including the contribution of Blessed Columba Marmion. Rome: Pontifical University of St. Thomas Aquinas. (Dissertation – STD).

United States Council of Catholic Bishops (USCCB). 2006. *Program of Priestly Formation, 5th ed.* Washington, DC.

van der Ven, J. 1998. Practical theology: an empirical approach. Trans. B. Schultz. Leuven: Peeters. Vanhoye, A. (2009). Aspetti fondamentali del sacerdozio nel nuevo testamento. *Seminarium*, 49(1):29–46.

Vatican Council II. 1964. *Lumen gentium.* Retrieved June 20, 2016, from http://www.vatican.va/archive/hist_councils/ii_vatican_council/documents/vat-ii_const_19641121_lumen-gentium_en.html.

Vatican Council II. 1965. *Presbyterorum ordinis.* Retrieved June 23, 2017 from http://www.vatican.va/archive/hist_councils/ii_vatican_council/documents/vat-ii_decree_19651207_presbyterorum-ordinis_en.html. Date of access: 26 May 2016. Latin text:

http://www.vatican.va/archive/hist_councils/ii_vatican_council/documents/vat-ii_decree_19651207_presbyterorum-ordinis_lt.html.

Wadell, P.J. 1995. The role of friendship in the moral and spiritual development of seminarians. *Seminary Journal*, 1(2), pp. 19-29.

Webb, R.J. 1999. Transitions into diocesan priesthood. *Seminary Journal*, 5(1), pp. 37-46.

Williamson, P.S. 2015. Spiritual foundations for the priest as beloved son. In Keating, J., Ed.., *The priest as beloved son*. Omaha, NE: IPF Publications, pp. 11-30.

Zlock, C. 2017. Decisions, direction and the "Disciple Maker Index." Retreived on November 30, 2017 from https://frzlock.com/2017/08/04/decisions-direction-and-the-disciple-maker-index-part-1/.

Zollner, H. 2005. Making life-decisions according to the Ignatian method of discernment (criteria). Retrieved August 1, 2019 from http://www.sjweb.info/documents/cis/pdfenglish/200511008en.pdf.

About the Author

Rev. Alfredo I. Hernández is Acting President-Rector of St. Vincent de Paul Regional Seminary in Boynton Beach, Florida, where he has served as Vice-Rector, Academic dean and a member of the formation faculty from 1997 to 1999 and from 2013 to the present.

Ordained a priest of the Diocese of Palm Beach in 1992, he served 14 years as Pastor of St. Juliana Parish in West Palm Beach, from 1999 to 2013, and a year as the director of permanent diaconate formation from 2015 to 2016.

He earned an STL in Dogmatic Theology from the Pontifical Gregorian University in Rome and a PhD in Pastoral Studies from North-West University in Potchefstroom, South Africa.

www.ingramcontent.com/pod-product-compliance
Lightning Source LLC
Chambersburg PA
CBHW022008090426
42741CB00007B/936

9781952464102